T0020932

THE BOOK OF EXPLANATIONS

THE BOOK OF EXPLANATIONS

Tedi López Mills

Translated by Robin Myers

DEEP VELLUM PUBLISHING
DALLAS, TEXAS

Deep Vellum Publishing
3000 Commerce St., Dallas, Texas 75226
deepvellum.org · @deepvellum

Deep Vellum is a 501c3 nonprofit literary arts organization
founded in 2013 with the mission to bring
the world into conversation through literature.

Copyright © 2012 by Tedi López Mills
Translation copyright © 2022 by Robin Myers
This edition published by arrangement with VF Agencia Literaria.
Originally published as *El libro de las explicaciones* by Editorial
Almadía in Mexico City, Mexico, in 2012
First Deep Vellum edition, 2022
All rights reserved.

No part of this book may be reproduced, or stored in a retrieval
system, or transmitted in any form or by any means, electronic,
mechanical, photocopying, recording, or otherwise, without express
written permission of the publisher.

The essay "On the Production of Wisdom" previously appeared in
The Spectacle.

ISBNs:
978-1-64605-125-0 (paperback)
978-1-64605-126-7 (ebook)

LIBRARY OF CONGRESS CONTROL NUMBER: 2022930833

Cover design by Jack Smyth
Interior Layout and Typesetting by KGT

PRINTED IN THE UNITED STATES OF AMERICA

CONTENTS

0.

IMPROPER NAMES

Et Socrates estime digne du soing paternel
de donner un beau nom aux enfans.

—Montaigne

1

It's my first day at a new elementary school in Mexico City. The teacher takes attendance:

"Hernández, Juan."

"Jiménez, Laura."

"Juárez, Adolfo."

"Lara, Pedro.

"López, Sandra."

"López, Tedi?"

I raise my hand, whisper *here*. Everyone turns to look at me.

"Let's see . . . there must be a mistake. What's your name?"

"Tedi."

"I'm sorry, Tedi? That's all? Tedi?"

"Yes . . ."

The other students stare, smiling. Some start to tease: Teddy, Teddy Bear . . .

"Well, you won't be Tedi in this class. We're going to call you Teodora. Teodora López."

And they did, at first. But Teodora was a dry name, a little too long, vowel-heavy, inappropriate for a ten-year-old girl. So the teacher set another rule.

"Teodora . . . well, all right, we'll call you Tedi, but just as a nickname for Teodora, okay? Is that clear, boys and girls?"

"Yes, Tedi, Teddy Bear, Tedi, Teddy Bear . . ."

"Okay, kids, that's enough."

What's the genre here? A tragicomedy, I'm tempted to suggest, although the repetition of this episode—at the start of every school year, every budding friendship, every social introduction, every official form, including one I filled out just yesterday—saps it of both comedy and drama, burdening it with the tedium of an official account that not even I entirely understand:

"How come that's your name?"

I had to ask my parents. Their explanation was a disaster, riddled with chronological blackouts. Only one thing was clear: my name wasn't an accident, an impulse, but a decision they'd meticulously deliberated in a moment of inspiration. To keep other people from assigning me a diminutive like Teresita, Susanita, Carmencita, Maruquita, Anita, etc., my dad said they'd opted to give me one themselves.

My mom intervened: "Yes, we named you Tedi after my brother Edward, who we called Teddy. But we Hispanicized it to avoid confusion."

My uncle Teddy, a pilot in World War II, had died in combat. He was the hero of my mother's family. Everyone missed Teddy, talked about Teddy, admired Teddy, and mourned Teddy, but it had never dawned on me that his death, many years before, was connected to my birth—to such an extent that my name and I had become a tribute to his interrupted life.

But so it was, and so it is. Surprisingly, revealing a stubbornness that doesn't quite suit my nature, I remain Tedi to this day—sometimes even Tedita. And I still answer the same question over and over: "What's the deal with your name?" At several critical junctures, I've resolved to take up a pseudonym. Once I said so to my mother and her eyes filled with tears: Tedi was going to betray *Teddy*. I felt terrible and didn't do it. Later, I tried out the initial: T. López Mills. But the abbreviation still subjected me to another form of the usual puzzlement: "What does 'T.' stand for?" Which immediately prompted the original question, and thus the same long answer as always. Over time, the details escaped me or disintegrated until I compressed them into a curt dismissal of my parents' odd, pointless attempt at originality.

It's not easy to get rid of a name. When I'd complain to my father, he'd always retort with the brief tale of Pedro Caca ("Pedro Poop"), who changed his name to Juan Caca (or the other way around). My dad found it hilarious, but I couldn't see what it had to do with my own predicament.

Sensing my confusion, he'd stop joking and speak to me seriously: "What would you like to be called? Would you rather have some ordinary little name like Diana, Adela, Alejandra?"

Exactly, I'd answer in my head. But how could I make such a confession to my father? He'd write me off as cowardly, simplistic. He was categorically at war with convention, and I wasn't eager to become another of his victims. So I kept being Tedi: now as an act of courage, of staunch individuality.

My conviction was frail. In my daydreams, sprawled across the living room couch or staring out at a tenuous horizon from the yard, my name was ideally Adriana or Claudia or Mónica, and I was still myself without the everyday nuisance of being me. The setting was different: another house (bigger), another car (newer), other parents, slightly better at being normal. I was pretty sure that you could get to the heart of an entire life based on the name of the person living it. And I was wholly confident of one thing: if I'd been called Marta or Isabel or Beatriz or Verónica, no one would have interrogated me about the origins of my name. And that in itself would rule out one possible path: the path of lingering in the threshold, asking "Why is this my name?" and hearing "Why is that your name?" Maybe a nominalist mystery can endure if it conceals a real mystery. But if there's just a simple person behind it, perhaps it's best to skip the obfuscation and start with something utterly clear. Something that puts the person first, rather than the banality or the eccentricity of her name, like a disguise she has to take off before she can share any kind of experience with anyone named—ah, utopia!—Álvaro or José or Alicia or Jimena.

But who am I scolding? No one. Or myself. For hesitating. Although, if you really can deduce a destiny from a name, maybe Tedi's didn't start with enough common sense. Maybe, like any other species, it was just trying to perpetuate itself, to persevere. Once created, Tedi decided to keep being Tedi. Alongside me. Despite the tragicomedy that morphs into a farce, once saturated with time and consciousness:

"What's your name?"

"Tedi."

"I'm sorry?"

"Tedi."

"Eddie?"

"No . . ."

"Terry?"

". . ."

"Oh, Terry! What a pretty name."

2

As a result of my general precariousness (or my fate), I cling to definitions. According to my dictionary of philosophy, Aristotle defined the name as "a vocal sound, significant by convention, independent of time, the parts of which are not significant when taken separately." And in *The Names of Christ*, Fray Luis de León writes that "the name, if we must designate it with a few words, is a brief word that replaces the one of which we speak and substitutes it for the same. The name is the very same as that which is named, not in the real and true being it possesses, but in the being which our mouth and understanding grant it."

Here lurks the notion of an unnameable essence. In simplistic terms: you can call a chair a chair, a table a table, a bench a bench, but doing so doesn't bring you into contact with their true selves. One's own name—I say this in my state of near anonymity—must contain even more essence than an ordinary word. Just imagine everything encompassed by Aristotle or Fray Luis de

León—an "everything" then mixed with their names. How can it be measured? I'm not sure if the amount of essence changes depending on the quality of the person. Nor do I know if souls keep their names in the actual Beyond. Saints don't seem to lose theirs. But maybe those names belong to us, not to them; in the Beyond, identity can't possibly rely on a convention, on a "vocal sound." There must be an immediate confirmation of who's who, and I can't imagine that anyone goes around asking "What's your name?" In the end, the essence says it all, unmediated.

But in the meantime, both before and after, we've got heaps of names. Elementally speaking, the Bible is a compendium of lineages whose members transcend convention by attaching themselves to tradition and a sacred, primordial trade. "Not only does God fit the names he grants with the essence of the named things in themselves," writes Fray Luis de León, "but also, whenever he has granted one and imbued it with some particular quality, in addition to those it already had, he has also granted some new name that corresponds to it." There, significant and signifying, are Moses and Abraham and Joshua and Esther and Miriam and Sarah and Ruth and Jacob and Jonas and Mary and Matthew and John and Peter. Ontologically envious, I imagine what it would be like to be represented by a name whose very first story is told in the book of all books. What distinguishes them from their essences? Maybe the nuance is numerical: how much person versus how much persona. The result of the operation wouldn't necessarily exclude the weight of the name. Here's my cynical, mystical wager: the less name there is (Tedi), the more persona (Teddy Bear), and therefore less essence (me). The path of askesis is revealed in all its radiance: a theology of proper names to purify the improper ones.

Traced this way, the circle tends toward viciousness. In "Cratylus," Plato's dialogue on language, Socrates and Hermogenes talk about names. Socrates, opposing relativism, insists that "it is necessary to name things as it is natural to name them, and to name them with the appropriate instrument, not according to our whims." The question arises at once: what instrument is that? Socrates offers several guidelines: to weave, one needs a shuttle; to bore, an auger. To name, then, what does one need? "A name," Hermogenes responds. "Perfectly," Socrates says. "And so the name is too an instrument." As with an auger or a shuttle, there must be an expert in handling the instrument of names. Who is it? The law, Socrates replies. "The legislator . . . the laborer of names," who knows how "to form with sounds and syllables the name that most naturally fits each thing; who forms and creates all names, affixing his gaze to the name itself."

Socrates is thinking out loud: there are no conclusions, only well-argued doubts. To conduct his inquiries, he draws from "Homer and the other poets." When names are virtuosic, they allude to motion, change, and flux. If not, if they convey stillness, stasis, stagnation; they are defective. But there is no alteration that may warp their essence: it doesn't matter much if one letter is replaced with another, one syllable with another, so long as the thing's essence dominates the name and is manifested there. Hermogenes concedes to Socrates, which is enough for Socrates to transform the hypothesis. In comes Cratylus, whom the reader has completely forgotten. On the surface, it seems like the three speakers agree. But Socrates turns things around again: "Do you not find some names better than others?" he asks Cratylus, who responds with total confidence: "No, all are names and all are proper." This uniformity is dissatisfying to Socrates, who points out that a name is one thing and the named object quite another; the name amounts to an imitation, and both good and bad imitations can exist. If the resemblance between names and objects were absolute, "everything would be done twofold . . . and it would be impossible to say: this is the thing and this is the name." Cratylus relents on this point, although he still believes that names reveal the nature of things and that the first legislators deduced the first designations. Socrates won't have it: if names show us the nature of things and one knows things by their names, then how could the first legislators have known them without their names? After all, "the first words did not exist, and . . . it is impossible to learn or discover things without having first learned or discovered for oneself the meaning of their names." Which is to say: things come before names, and you can get to know them in themselves and by yourself without their assistance. The dialogue ends somewhere else: if nothing lasts, then what can we know? Socrates asks Cratylus to investigate the problem and inform him of any truth he should uncover. Each carries on along his path, or his tangent. Each, it seems to me, with his own proper name—which must affect the plot of the essence, or at least of the story.

3

There's hope. According to the Socratic argument, beings are over here and their names are over there. Or, to quote Fray Luis de León once again: "There are two forms or two differences of names: some that inhabit the soul and others that sound in the mouth." In this double life, maybe *Tedi* is a shoddy imitation of me, even if I'm forced to acknowledge that something *tediesque* about my essence may have prompted it. Maybe the first syllable, *Te*, hit the mark, and then my parents' deductive capacity faltered for ideological reasons, erasing what was to follow: *re-sa*, *o-do-ra*, or *o-re-ma*.

In my own speculative experiments, I've thought I felt—and that's exactly the verb I mean—that I fit just fine into the shape of Teresa. I've thought I wouldn't even mind being called Tere, or, worse yet, Teresita. The obstacle, though, is the inner life, the current of consciousness, where I'd struggle to replace each apparition of Tedi with Teresa, where it would unsettle me to scold myself with another name: as if there were someone other than myself in me. I'd have to keep being Tedi inside and Teresa outside. Although, if it's true that a name is a destiny, maybe this would trigger an identity conflict: a war of names that Teresa would surely win. All too late, I'd understand that Tedi really was me.

There must be archives of bad names somewhere: records of their silly legends, farces in lieu of myths. Then we could prove that improper names ultimately infiltrate our essences and sap value from the authentic I. And then it wouldn't matter if Tedi turned into Teresa, because her particular I is a surface that has already been interfered with, as it were. Surely, in such archives, there must also be a folder of texts penned by the poorly named, or by their compassionate scribes. Texts that try to reclaim the solemnity of the life behind its outlandish nomenclature, legends of faintly hysterical someones who sought to churn out traditions for their names; who hoped their names would put down roots and propagate and stabilize. Or maybe that's how it happened with all good names at first: first risible and extravagant, then normal and opportune. In my own silly legend, I've imagined the glorious moment when some friend decides to name their daughter Tedi and my name acquires its first bright coat of orthodoxy. Maybe, a couple Tedis down the line, the design flaw will start to fade, and as the years pass, Tedi will appear in some brief appendix to the official list of names.

I keep postponing my decision. Tedi or Teresa? According to A., it's already too late. But he speaks from the perfection of his name. For someones like me, time passes in a marginal, anomalous way, and this winding path can still be righted. If I were to opt for Teresa, I'd do away with the López and the Mills, softening the betrayal of both Teddy and Tedi. I'd choose an allusive surname: Lobo, say. Teresa Lobo. I shared this scenario with a friend, who looked at me with mild condescension (peering down from his most proper of names) and asked if he could keep calling me Tedi. I thought of Sisyphus pushing his boulder uphill every day, only to have it roll all the way down each time. Being Teresa only to stay Tedi forever. A. recommends a more logical alternative: return to Teodora but keep the López. That way I'd maintain an aural, retrospective, vital, social bond with Tedi. Because of the essences and whatnot. With any luck, we won't lose what's in our soul to change what sounds in the mouth.

1.

ON HOW TIME PASSES,
IN CONSCIOUSNESS AND OUTSIDE

The sentence I type, my fingers moving over the keys, the pause, my breath, my distraction, the fly darting into my studio, the phone ringing in another room, the birds outside, the plane overhead, my cat slipping in and out, my cat asleep, etc., even the etc. itself in this sequence, occur in time, and, worse yet, in their own sphere of time, which barely resembles my own, which is stating the obvious, but which is also, at least for me, a paradox, in that if I stopped to study it, it would become a locus of distress, because, once again, the parts that make up the paradox, the words I use to express it or explain it, also occur in time, and if I tried to reveal how they work or solve the mystery, I'd have to take it all apart until the fragments of the entire artifact were shunted aside, piled up in the margins, and I, also in the margins, would then be able to review them all before a single minute had passed; then the fragments and I would rejoin the current, certain that time and the idea of time are one and the same and can't be expressed without introducing another line of succession: an after *that* before. And so it would be in every single case. Like, for example, the case of this text or essay or log I'm writing: I'd formulated several possible beginnings in my mind, and so the start was still the stuff of chance, but as soon as I set down the first word, a path began to unfurl that no longer depends much on me and what I meant or on my choice of opening line.

I don't know how possible it is to redirect this kind of fate. The first paragraph must have already split a fissure in the time of time; everything that follows will ultimately settle into its contours. But this doesn't exclude my intervention or invalidate the also-temporal fact that I jotted down two parallel starting points yesterday:

A.
A friend once told me that the only thing he had against making love was the duration . . .

B.
Borges once said in an interview that he didn't like traveling; he liked the fact of having traveled . . .

I'll intervene—or take a liberty—by advancing both beginnings. I should add that everything that happens will happen in *real time.*

A.

A friend once told me that the only thing he had against making love was the duration. When sex goes on for a while, the once-spontaneous movement of the two bodies seems to grow conscious of itself, to observe itself from outside: noisy, sweaty, mechanical. And then my friend would be pierced by an awareness of imminent boredom, the threat of time obstructing intimacy as it passed, and he'd ask an anxious question: "Did you come?" If she said no, my friend would feel like yelling or crying, but he'd gallantly carry on, grappling and enduring until he'd heard her final snarl; brusquely, he'd come, too, then roll off her body, light a cigarette, and sigh with gratitude: the fiction was over. By contrast, if she said yes, he'd kiss her, gently let himself go, then sweetly drop to one side and say with tenderness, almost with love, "That was wonderful," before lighting his cigarette.

My friend explained the problem to me. Consciousness sometimes fell into a trap, overlapping with what he felt as he felt it, joining the action, six-guns blazing: "Now I'm caressing, kissing, pumping in, pumping out, grasping, gripping, I'm seeing myself doing it, I'm seeing that she's seeing me do it, I'm seeing myself seeing her, I'm seeing her seeing me, I want what I'm in the middle of to be over so I can re-lose my awareness of what I'm experiencing." For my friend, brevity was a decisive influence on the quality (and sincerity) of his feelings. Only when it came to sex, he claimed; other pleasures may commit the sin of duration, but consciousness doesn't rear up like an obstacle to consummating that pleasure. That is, perception doesn't inhibit experience. Which is false. I suspect my friend wanted to boast an erotic jadedness that would have identified him with authors in vogue at the time: Klossowski, Bataille, and their more tiresome predecessor, the Marquis de Sade. My friend cultivated sexual boredom as a form of philosophical lucidity and seduction.

I don't doubt his candor. In the end, my friend had a heightened sense of time and was easily bored. Maybe that's why he always talked more than was strictly necessary and concocted elaborate theories to entangle the simplest ideas. Once I dared suggest that consciousness ruins almost everything: walking, running, going up or down stairs, dancing, thinking, laughing. Which is why the problem isn't time, but consciousness, ourselves, the I. Or the problem lies in treating time as a presence that exists apart from us and which we invoke, not the very substance we inhabit. Although "presence" and "substance" already have a certain esoteric ring to them. Where do we exist—or, better put, where do we become? I think I am someone to me, but when I appeal to what I call my consciousness in hopes of determining its identity, time stops and I vanish, like a skittish animal. Consciousness, therefore, is an impediment to observing consciousness, which is a current of perceptions and happenings, of time that goes on and on unless we decide to puncture it with the hook of self-knowledge: the river disappears and I am revealed as a hazy surface.

It strikes me as acceptable, if barely reasonable, that time doesn't need my consciousness in order to carry on in my head (where my consciousness supposedly lives). What I find far more troubling is that I isn't needed for me to be myself, that my consciousness doesn't need me: in fact, it freezes when I gather the nerve to ask it about me or it. Who lives inside me, then, as the lead actor in my persona? I'd say it's I: in the third person, ironically. Someone dressed up as I, oblique, staring straight ahead. No one. "For my part," writes David Hume in the essay on personal identity that appears in *A Treatise of Human Nature*, "when I enter most intimately into what I call myself, I always stumble on some particular perception or other, of heat or cold, light or shade, love or hatred, pain or pleasure. I never can catch myself at any time without a perception, and never can observe any thing but the perception." According to Hume, we are nothing but an accumulation of perceptions, and we never even catch a glimpse of our own identity—simply, directly—as something constant and unchanging. Imagination (whose, mine? not I but I would ask) invents the feeling of identity. As a result, our perception of variable and invariable objects feels like a single uninterrupted action, and thus "we run into the notion of a soul, and self, and substance, to disguise the variation." In other words, identity is a sensation produced by the imagination's steady course. Which clarifies nothing, and in fact is only startling, even terrifying: someone or something inside us, inside myself, is asking the questions; someone or something wants to get to know itself, wants to know; there is some element or mechanism at work in consciousness that suddenly wakes up and asks itself, who am I, what is time? Something or someone formulates the questions that Hume answers in first person when he writes "For my part, I . . ."

The French philosopher Clément Rosset lays out the matter far more dramatically in his book *Loin de moi: étude sur l'identité* (*Far From Me: A Study on Identity*). Only social identity is real, writes Rosset, while the other identity, the personal one, is just an illusion: "total and . . . persistent." But who protects that illusion? In Rosset's view, the "I" is an invisible guest, or a visible one "from a line of sight that prevents me from looking it in the eye and identifying it for sure." He doesn't explain who houses the guest. Let's say it's the body, which means there's a bodily function that asks questions—questions that throw a wrench in the gears. The whole substance of the "I," adds Rosset, comes from a "you" (who, by the way, also believes itself to be an "I"). And introspection is a contradiction: the "I" can't take itself up as an object of study; "a lens can't observe itself." Rosset's conclusion is distressing: we know ourselves only in relation to others. And who is each of us when we're alone? Just a guest who comes and goes.

Modestly, "I" would suggest another ongoing dilemma: the existence of moods. My friend's boredom (or panic) when sex dragged on, pulling him into the uncomfortable shadows where two bodies act like ridiculous objects because consciousness has intervened: who does it belong to? Who is the subject of all actions, including the subject's negation? Heidegger theorized that moods distinguish us from being. Conscious time can be equated to a mood. If I forget myself, time passes more quickly, for better or worse. Or the other way around: I forget myself precisely because it's passing quickly. There are special intervals when, at least for me, consciousness and time flow along harmoniously, although the two are never identical. For example, when I abstain from all activity, when I sit or lie down, I drift, I let myself be carried along, I think a thought, remember, watch the light in the window, the shape of the tree outside, the blots of rain on the glass, I think again, remember something else, hear distant noises, stare up at the ceiling, sigh, perhaps, and return; five or seven minutes may have passed on the clock, hours or eons or thousands of instants in my head. Another example: the rare occasions when I try to meditate, the even rarer ones when I actually do. I sit in lotus position, my hands at my sides; I close my eyes and seek a center in my mind, and place myself there, and immediately push out the contents of my mind to carve a hollow and allow the world, life, the self, whatever you want to call it, to circulate through me, unobstructed by my persona; I pretend I'm not, I listen to the elements, until my bent knees beg for mercy and I open my eyes and return to myself. Curiously, sheer inertia brings me to be who I am. But the opposite, the absence of identity—which for some mysterious reason Hume defends and Rosset insists on proving at all costs—is something I must force in a deliberate act of self-cancellation. In other words: I am by instinct; I'm just another sense; or, baroquely, I'm the sense of senses. And nonbeing, absence, that space in the center of my mind when I wipe it clean, isn't silence, but a continuous current of sounds. As soon as I hear myself, I stop hearing them. Maybe that's the proof that I exist: my own noise. Although it doesn't ensure me the exactitude of an I: which is a conjugation, a grammatical structure, Hume would say. But so is he, I would add, and so are they and so are you and so are we. No one is spared from being a word.

And no paradox, no show of false innocence, can solve my friend's quandary when sex dillydallies, and time turns into consciousness, and bodies are inserted into hyperrealism, and such is their weight that pleasure becomes repulsion and sends out a swift shoot of existentialism and a crude insinuation that boredom is somehow deep or philosophical. How much longer now? There are not three times, Saint Augustine suggested, but three presents: the present of the past, the present of the present, and the present of the future. My friend always got stuck in the second on his way to the third, where he'd try to remember the first. Eternity would have been unbearable to him, if it hadn't been so brief.

B.

Borges once said in an interview that he didn't like traveling; he liked the fact of having traveled. This is a metaphor for time and a parable of returns and a "mobile image" of the circle itself, since a straight line would distance a person from the point where she paused to contemplate the ground she'd already covered and the ground yet to be covered; it would extend, by nature, both backward and forward. Or at least that's what I imagine: corrupted, surely, by the cartoons I've seen again and again, where time is a line that stretches on whenever you stop. Toward infinity, or toward an earthly shore. Which is why it's reckless to leave wherever you happen to be: which point along the line will you return to? In my sketch, it would be a little before and a little after wherever I started out from, and only to the same place if the miracle of cyclical time should suddenly triumph.

Borges's phrase also betrays a preference: for nostalgia. Travel is full of so many static minutes that the engines only rev up after the fact, when you remember. Remembering, you'll finally embark on the trip that was impossible in situ, because the trip itself obstructed you. You reach your destination, check in at your hotel or hostel, carry your luggage upstairs, unpack, look at yourself in the bathroom mirror, re-confirm that no mirror is identical to any other, go back down to the lobby, and wonder, "Now what do I do with the rest of this day or afternoon or night?" Everyday life is out of the picture. You are the master of your time and almost everything, except for uncertainty, shifts into the future. The only way to truly experience what you've already experienced is when you return home and start remembering. Only then will the trip assume the order of a discrete, indelible adventure—an order it never had at the time, because you were constantly deliberating over a series of options. The present you encountered in the lobby was actually an array of different futures that, afterward, in the reminiscing mind, will become mere compilations of the past. "Memory tends toward the timeless . . ." writes Borges in A History of Eternity; "the differently red sunsets I see every evening will become, in my memory, a single sunset." Much to the relief of consciousness, which pretends that the past is eternal and nostalgia a numerical operation that subdivides it into stages and sensations, as if telling a story before regaining its composure, and as if the story included its own motionlessness: life lived as a space where statues enact the marble blocks that promise them the shape they already have. And this shouldn't be understood, because precise, linear time decreed that the rules would change, and that, instead of remembering, our consciousness would fashion equations out of the scraps.

And what about me? I'll do an experiment: I'll reconstruct a trip, piecing together my memories, to see where reality ended up. I can already make out the molds where my feelings will fit into place. While I can remember the most trivial details (long highway drives through a monotonously beautiful landscape, indecisive walks down a sidewalk in search of a restaurant), my nostalgia starts to assemble its own account: the impeccable journey of the past.

Not long ago, I went—we went—to the Grand Canyon. There was a snowstorm during our three-day stay and the canyon, always cloaked in thick, flat clouds, was barely visible. The cold was cutting, painful. Every excursion meant subjecting ourselves to the frigid damp, the frost-glazed ground, the biting wind, in order to peer over the narrow, dizzying brink; to glimpse, through the mist, the river's smeary zigzag and the white earth with its red patches at the top; to exclaim with the other tourists, sigh at the beauty, etc. Then the analogies: "The Grand Canyon is like a group of huge abandoned temples, don't you think?" The silence of its abyss was intensified by the silence of the snow, which an over-flying crow occasionally disrupted; "Look how black it is"; a sudden sunbeam tore into the emptiness below, and for a moment we could see all the way to the bottom, among bushes and boulders; *If I tried to find the echo*, I thought, but I didn't dare shout in the presence of so many people; beside me, an elderly man beheld the chasm and remarked to his wife, "And to think that there are still people who refuse to believe in God . . ."; once again, the cold lash against my face forced me to close my eyes and reopen them quickly, so that my eyelids wouldn't freeze shut; the mind inside doesn't recognize this temperature or understand where to file it, other than under the general category of pain; "Let's go inside," I say, ashamed, and I promise myself to remember this view forever while I imagine the comfort of a roof overhead.

I go out into the white night for a cigarette and snuff it in the snow with my boot and a crunch under the heel makes me grasp for another analogy: when I step on snow it sounds like: snow when I step on it; tautology, because my mind can't summon a comparable noise. Does that say something about me or about the snow? I don't mind the cold if the smoke precedes the comparisons between my body and a stone shattering one slow blow at a time. Afterward, in the restaurant, I brood on the fact that thinking about the world separates me from the world and I sink into a kind of nocturnal ataxia: what do I say now?; "Let's go," I urge, ashamed again, and we retreat to our hotel along a path paved with gravel and snow and I'm sure I'll never forget this rigid, unswerving cold, clear as the lack of color throughout our stay.

A trip conceals another trip. How to know which is real and which is the material of recollection? According to Hume, memory is the origin of personal identity: not by producing that identity, but by discovering it. And so, as a strict logical derivation, I wasn't *I* during my travels; I was witness to a chain of circumstances that would later become a memory starring my own persona. Back home after the trip, sitting or lying down or walking through my neighborhood, with my memory flung open to the natural course of reconstruction, I see myself crossing the snowy meadow beside the void of the

Grand Canyon, my head spooled in a scarf, the sky livid with snowflakes falling as slowly as leaden drops. I see myself hurrying for shelter, thinking about how travel is always uncomfortable because reality always interferes and it's better to remember a trip as a convergence with the present: "This reminds me of that day at the Grand Canyon when . . ." And the passing of time in your consciousness is the point where one end of the past is tied to a loose thread of the present and their union sparks a shock in you—nostalgia, maybe, which would be proof that you exist, at least in reverse.

Borges once wrote that eternity isn't conceivable, "but neither is humble linear time." I suppose we experience the linear and long for its opposite; that is, we live within purely inconceivable coordinates, within consciousness and beyond it. Which is why there are clocks (and, for some humans, cats, which are the masters of our habits or their inventors; when my cat comes into the room, I know it's time, I get up, and although I may not know which clock marked the hour or where, my watch unmistakably strikes twelve).

2.

IMAGINATION TURNED
INTO MEMORY

A.

Lately, when I imagine, I remember. Then I shift into a peaceful kind of forgetfulness. And I start to imagine again, remembering. Like a circle that's no longer vicious because it erases its own trail, little by little, always re-sketching its outline for the first time.

B.

Yesterday I dreamed of an ice rink and a frozen staircase. It wasn't a compelling dream; the symbolism of the white and the cold and the clumsy skates twisting on the ice with my feet inside them struck me as so ordinary that I decided to interpret it literally. And not even that was enough to hold my attention.

In the morning I retold the dream so I'd have something to tell and could assign an anecdote to the night itself, which was long and uncomfortable and full of bodies. My dreams never come from my imagination; they're the recycling of my most elemental memories.

Today is less predictable than yesterday was. Who knows what the night will bring. The raindrops on the windowpane are as rigid as routine. As soon as I focus on them, they lose their rhythm, sound arbitrary.

C.

Maybe I remember when I imagine because I'm already starting to forget.

I'd like to know what I'm going to forget. Or is it what I imagine? But then forgetting would be some intricate procedure in which you'd have to decipher the stuff of imagination in order to recover the memories that, adding insult to injury, you don't even recognize anymore—because you've forgotten them. Which means you perceive them as original images. Shreds of memory that could gradually amass into a creative form of amnesia. An extravagant thriller: the protagonist is the only character who never shows up.

No matter how hard I try not to, I stumble into labyrinths. It must be the natural path of aimless words: they immediately assemble the artifice of a style. And in a labyrinth, the surface is just as complex as the depths are.

D.

There are corpses.

If I know what I forget, I remember everything. I'm Funes:[1] someone paralyzed by the weight of my memory, and then, if I'm lucky, by everyone else's memory, too. That's why it doesn't grant me a gender, which is crucial these days. What's most truly mine, I suspect, what lies beneath my skin, is neutral. Unfortunately, its claim of innocence is worth little. It's said that any gender — any genre — is guilty of excluding all the rest. But I'd suggest that neutrality doesn't exclude, precisely because it doesn't include. So who feels the caresses? Their memory, which imagines them as soon as it forgets.

E.

In my imagination of this newly arrived memory, there's a little girl, a garden, a house full of birds in the middle of the garden, and three windows set into the gray walls. The girl, kneeling, scrapes a red brick until she produces a very fine dust, the proofreader of my memories would add, wanting all recollections to be beautiful, spiritual.

---

1. "Funes el memorioso," or "Funes the Memorious," is a story by Jorge Luis Borges in which the protagonist acquires the gift, or curse, of prodigious memory.

F.

It bothers me that they insist on being fragments: as if my consciousness were too small for them.

Although I'm not sure if they take place in my consciousness, or if they even take place at all: maybe they float because they're dying. The unconscious will be their amphitheater.

G.

I don't remember my first memory.

In my second memory, I'm watching my baby brother kick his feet as my mother wipes his buttocks and legs. This memory is theirs, not mine.

Or, in Freudian terms, it could be interpreted as the beginning of the end of a reign: my brother will replace me in my mother's arms.

A perfect, boring schema: I remember because it was the origin of a trauma; my brother doesn't remember because it was the beginning of guilt.

But that's not how it is, because it's not any way at all. I choose chance: the memories that remain, whether my own or someone else's, are the ones that successfully seep through. The others, fragile, are forgotten: the theory of evolution as applied to memory.

Although this contradicts the hypothesis of dying memories. Chance permits it. The only rule is to keep playing: remembering.

H.

Memory is proof—fragile as an article of faith—of my existence over time.

I could ask someone else for evidence: "Wasn't I here with you the day before yesterday?" If confirmed, the knot of fear will loosen. If not, paranoia will unfurl in the opposite direction until it attaches to the first memory, which is the first forgetfulness, biting its own tail as soon as it remembers.

I.

There were two trees in my memory. A long river. There were little girls' bodies struggling against the frigid water. There was a pond farther up, rough ground, wet rocks. There was an older girl in the pond and the little ones watching, waiting. "Take off your clothes," they told her. The girl pulled off her shirt and the little girls went quiet. It was in their eyes, the silence. The little girls' hands wanted to touch but the water was too far away.

J.

I can't get used to forgetting. I see the holes in what's slipping away.

I guess they'll close up eventually and I'll only know what I remember, without the crutch of dialectics.

K.

In my memory of this moment, there's a room with a bunk bed. I'm on the bottom mattress; up top is an English boy who smells bad. I'm excited by the fact that he's English and smells bad; it makes me feel interesting. The English boy has long hair and speaks in a very low voice. Suddenly he announces that he wants to leave. He peers over the edge to look at me. I make a face I'd never made before.

It's a memory that includes a memory: my own face.

L.

You can play a very basic game of chess with paving tiles in the street. This is what I do when I remember how I used to play chess in hopes of impressing an invisible audience: I'd furrow my brow and never win.

Will today manage to become a memory?

(In another life, he's an ephebe I would have liked to put into my head: an ephebe of ideas and of the heart.)

M.

On Saturday I found myself somewhere dark at three in the afternoon. There were tiny servings of food on enormous plates. We all exclaimed "They're like abstract paintings!" and laughed at the reference and talked about Nazis and feelings of guilt, about how long they last or how long they should last, about whether new poetics even exist or whether they're the same as always, ancient, just bloodier, about mothers who had already died or were beginning to die, about stories so perfect they don't even need to be written.

I went downstairs to the restroom and said to myself, "I won't forget this."

We left and emerged onto the street; there were lots of people milling around a fair full of trinkets in a park. We could hear the racket of the rides. One was a dragon that swayed in the air like a noisy, monotonous swing. Children shouted and parents clapped.

The fair wasn't included in what I wasn't going to forget. Maybe someday it will help me remember.

N.

The smell of grass always leads me to a memory.

In one of them, I'm lying on my back and looking for shapes in the clouds. I'd been told that this was what you were supposed to do when you lie on your back and look up at the sky. But I can't find any shapes. Sometimes I pretend and shout "A flower!" I'm almost always distracted by my own image: looking at myself look.

In another recollection, I'm rolling down a hill and someone named Tote is waiting for me at the bottom, where there's an abandoned cabin and a chimney covered with dry leaves.

In my memory, the grass is an automatic reflection: it turns on and arranges minimalist images across the screen, with the bygone rhythm of slides.

My grass conceals another stretch of grass, then another, until it reaches the first, which I've already forgotten so I can remember the next.

O.

Today I watched my cat remembering. A glimmer. I was in it.

P.

In my visions of fear, there's a man in profile. I know who he is but I can't remember him. If I'd forgotten him, why is he still there?

A taxi driver and I speak intensely about the weather; we try to remember the first heat wave that unleashed the subsequent heat waves and we peer backward, searching for the year, and we smile at each other in his rearview mirror because neither of us can find it.

This will be a repetition, not a memory.

Q.

I heard the alarm clock and the water at the same time.

I remember an American man shouting into a pay phone in a Sanborns café. Nearby, I'm seated at a table with someone I never saw again because the hang-ups of admiration spoiled the outcome. I tried to arrange some words alongside other words, but my friend only wanted to please me, and this inflamed my sense of adjacent loneliness.

The American weeps, cajoles: "Let me come back... please let me come back . . . you can't do this to me . . ." He's tall and fat; he looks like my high school gym teachers. My friend and I stop speaking.

There's another memory inside the memory: a little boy vomits on the stairs at the Atayde circus. I'm climbing them with my father and the tickets he's just bought. When we get home, I tell my father I don't want to go to the circus anymore and I lock myself in my room.

R.

I've strayed from memory: my self-compassion is a form of idolatry. Why am I consoling myself?

S.

My memory tries to get in the middle so it can capture forgetfulness as soon as it strikes.

T.

The content empties out very quickly. The image of the pink flamingos at night, flocking back to their refuge, is so canonically beautiful that it doesn't resize itself to fit my memories. I couldn't say that it belongs to me, but to the bird species and to humans engaging in a pantheistic experience: a chain effect of memories that never ends and is always someone else's. Or an epiphany, like what Joyce had. I wouldn't be able to distinguish them from a vision. The flamingos cloaked the dusk with their wings and their cries and I thought about how someday I'd tell someone about it as a recollection and how that someone would tell me, astonished, "You have such great memories."

U.

There was a dripping jar of honey, open, full of ants, in the kitchen of the cluttered apartment, its windows dim with grime. The tenant explained that the jar of honey and the ants scared off cockroaches.

This is a memory that someone else remembered in front of me yesterday.

Which reminds me of Brodsky's worst poem: "Buenas noches. / Don't mind the roaches."

V.

My brother hides under the bed because I'm chasing him and hunting him and his face is hurt from the car accident when he was flung against the windshield and splinters of glass were embedded in his forehead and nose and he's frightened, weeping under the bed, and I mock him.

This shouldn't be forgotten.

W.

I'm going to be taught a lesson in objective fear. It's a stain that fades when you study it up close. It looks like a red boulder when you follow the curve of the highway in a dream.

I'm going to be taught a lesson in putting myself in others' shoes and accepting the existence of empathy despite everything.

Later I'll remember and I'll feel a sense of peace about how good I was before I shut myself up in my head with memory's autopilot turning in incessant circles.

X.

Today my memory screeched to a halt. The last thing I saw was the plaza with a clown, children everywhere, myself among them.

Y.

It was supposed to be one day and became another. It's impossible to speak aloud.

I'd rather my imagination bump around inventing things than immerse itself in a formula without resources. Today I'll excommunicate it.

Sometimes, when nothing comes out of nowhere like a headlong sun, I run into Mr. Stetson in the supermarket aisles. I make a secret gesture to him that he immediately understands. I never ask him the crucial question: "Excuse me, weren't you with me in the ships at Mylae?"

Impossible in the supermarket at four in the afternoon.

But I've been in some ships. I remember.

Z.

Forgive my sins of negligence and ignorance.

Or I won't forgive yours.

3.

PORTRAIT OF A READER
AS A YOUNG WOMAN

For my friends

For Judy

DID THIS HAPPEN TO ME?

On the cusp of fourteen, where this story, this chronicle, this essay begins, desire moves faster than events do. At that age, almost nothing happens beyond your everyday routine and your major quandaries hinge on the decision between staying home or going out. The only real difference is how disappointed you feel in the minutes before you fall asleep, protesting: outside, boredom is a consequence, not a condition.

Pascal must be right: the world would be a better place, a more peaceful place, if none of us went anywhere. Which would be possible if there were no weekends, although instinct would invariably propose them anyway. The feeling lurks as early as Thursday night. The expectation. At age fourteen, you feel an urgent, anxious optimism as you await your itinerary. Any potential plan affects the quality of the experience. And the experience never transcends the plan, but it can still be ruined if you fail to brainstorm a proper sequence of activities on Thursdays with your friends. We'll get a ride to your house after school and after lunch we'll call Rafael and his friends. We'll go to a party and then we'll see.

Those are the instructions you give your own life. On Fridays, it's harder to get a ride home: you have to wait, which means you have to smoke, sitting on the sidewalk near the red gate; smoke and watch the others get into their cars and drive away. Until one girl finally says: We're going with so-and-so. You guys can take the bus. And it takes longer and longer to make it home for lunch, and when Rafael is finally called around six thirty, he isn't there. A message is left. Time to wait again. With every ring of the phone, it feels like the problem is about to be solved, but it's always someone else. At nine, then, the TV is switched on, and one of your girl-friends rolls a joint as another shuffles the cards for a game called war that never ends.

Saturday is usually less imperfect. It has the advantage of starting from the beginning. Rafael calls around noon and you plan to meet up later with him and his friends: Toño, Fernando, and two other boys whose names no one can ever remember. The next hours pass in front of the mirror, trying on clothes and a little makeup. There's competition: all the girls want to end up with Rafael or Toño, although they acknowledge that

Fernando is the nicest. The friend, the confidant, the good guy, the one you talk to whenever Rafael and Toño take turns paying attention to the others. Fernando listens as the displaced girls smoke, pretending that it doesn't matter.

The meeting place is a chain restaurant called Vips, or, rather, outside a Vips, by Rafael's car. That's the site of the first flirtations, and where the night's plans are drawn up: there's a party with a cover charge in Las Lomas, a new disco in the Zona Rosa, another party—a free one—at the house of an acquaintance in Coyoacán, a new taco place on División del Norte. Each option is discussed at great length and eventually discarded. What time is it, someone asks. Almost seven . . . And still nothing is decided. The girls' bodies tell the story of the boys' gaze. Rafael jokes, Toño smiles as if he always knew something no one else did, Fernando doles out cigarettes. The other two boys fade into the background and then disappear. Four girls, three boys. Finally they settle on the great adventure: driving in circles around Chapultepec Park in Rafael's car and then going for a taco or sandwich before calling it a night.

Rafael starts his car and the girls let out a shriek of freedom. One sits up front, between Rafael and Toño; the other three are in the back, the youngest perched on Fernando's knees. Did you bring any weed? Yeaaah . . . exclaim the voices in unison, the wind rushing in

through the open windows. Rafael drives fast. One of
the girls in the back gets scared and Fernando consoles
her. Don't worry, he says. She clenches her fists and
smiles. The front-seat girl urges him to go faster and
lights the first joint. The tires screech on the curves.
The girl who's scared stops talking. They pass her the
joint. She doesn't inhale. Better to get lost in her heart-
beat than in the smoke. She seeks shelter in the pulse:
how many thuds per minute. She focuses on listening
to herself from the inside. Toño puts on some music.
The front-seat girl sings along to the Doobie Brothers.
They're in the park now and Rafael slows down. Stop
there, up by that tree over there, says the front-seat girl.
She's so stoned, thinks the scared girl in back.

No one gets out of the car, no one speaks, no one
moves. The music is a cage. The scared girl feels hot
and clammy. She looks at Rafael's head: his long hair
still stirred by residual wind. She watches how Rafael
turns to kiss the neck of the front-seat girl and how
Toño notices too and opens the car door to get out. It's
a tacit order. Let's go, girls, Fernando says. And they all
get out except for Rafael and the front-seat girl, who are
kissing. The scared girl feels dizzy, on the verge of tears.
The other girls smoke and stare out at the pathways
through the trees. Fernando and Toño set out on one
of the trails. Don't go, don't leave us here, the girls say,
following the boys to another tree deeper in. Fernando

and Toño sit down on the ground, leaning against the trunk, and the girls arrange themselves around them. Fernando tells them a string of jokes until their laughter empties out into a troublesome silence. The scared girl imagines Rafael and her friend in the car: his tongue in her mouth and his hands under her shirt or near her underpants, a finger about to slip between her legs. Will she let him? Would the scared girl let him? I'm hungry, says the other girl. Let's go, it's awful here, and they stand up and head to the car. Toño raps on the window and Rafael turns, startled. He rolls it down: What's up, man . . . Well, the girls want to leave. Come on . . . You can finish up later . . . Rafael and the front-seat girl both laugh.

An imaginary steam begins to sediment inside the car. The scared girl thinks she smells something and asks Fernando to roll his window farther down. The racket of the wind is better than talking. Where are we going? she hears Toño ask. To get some food, right? Fernando responds. The front-seat girl rolls another joint and passes it around. These decisions always take forever. How much cash do you have on you? the scared girl hears. Not much, man, you? Me neither, but if we pool what we've got we can buy maybe two or three sandwiches . . . The front-seat girl shouts, Yeah, and we can eat them at my house . . .

They sing on the way to the sandwich place. The

scared girl perks up and studies Toño's neck. The girl beside her sings in a soft voice, barely a murmur. Rafael drives quietly. The front-seat girl proposes another song: "I'm a Believer!" Fernando protests: No way, not the fucking Monkees, never! The scared girl thinks of a Creedence song, but she doesn't say anything because everyone, except for Rafael, is talking all at once.

They set the sandwiches in the middle of the dining room table and cut them into pieces. The front-seat girl's parents call her upstairs and she goes to reassure them. *No worries, they're almost asleep ... I told them you'd leave after the sandwiches.* Having stopped at the bathroom, the scared girl arrives late to the table and ends up next to Fernando. Toño is talking with the other girl, laughing with her. Rafael and the front-seat girl give each other butterfly kisses and he tongues the crumbs from her lips. The scared girl's head starts to buzz and she can't make out what Fernando is telling her. From the corner of her eye, she sees Toño stroking the other girl's hair.

They go out into the yard and light another joint. The scared girl pretends to inhale and passes it to the other girl, the youngest, who takes a drag and says she's ready for bed. Where? The bedroom. It's almost midnight. Toño and the other girl walk to the back of the yard, their arms around each other; Rafael and the front-seat girl share pot smoke with a kiss; Fernando looks down at the ground and grabs the scared girl's hand. She smiles at him and says, I'll be right back . . . And just then, the parents' bedroom window opens. Yes, Dad, they're leaving, they're leaving . . .

The plan is very simple, and it works. The girls make a rowdy show of saying goodbye to the boys, but the boys are actually waiting outside, in Rafael's car. The girls go through the motions of setting up camp in the living room, they troop upstairs for blankets, the front-seat girl lets her parents know that the other two are sleeping over, her parents mumble a sleepy okay— and half an hour later, the girls open the door and sneak the boys into the house on tiptoe and they all file into the living room, where everything is ready.

The scared girl lies down on the couch. Toño and the other girl walk out into the garden with a blanket draped around their shoulders. Rafael and the front-seat girl sprawl out on the carpet, whispering as they rearrange cushions and covers. Fernando inches over to the scared girl and sits on the edge of the couch. She says her head and stomach hurt and she just wants to sleep. Fernando strokes her hair and forehead. She closes her eyes and turns away. Fernando lies down and puts his arm around her. I'll take care of you, he says. The scared girl doesn't answer. Little by little, she starts to calm down— Fernando doesn't try to do anything—and drifts off.

–

Rafael's voice wakes her: *Aaaahhh, oh, like that?* And the front-seat girl responds: *No, wait, I'll put it in, ow, wait, there, right there . . . ow . . . it hurts . . . ohh.* And Rafael: *Don't move, let it get in all the way . . . ooof . . . yeah . . . ahhh . . .* Then some grunts and the front-seat girl, with a tiny faltering laugh: *Careful, they'll hear us.* Rafael's breathing is choppy and the scared girl hears his body moving up and down and the silence of the front-seat girl and the snores of Fernando beside her, his arm still resting on her hip. She tries to be even more absolutely still. Suddenly the front-seat girl lets out a muted moan and Rafael grunts harder and collapses with a sigh, *ay mamita . . .* and the front-seat girl laughs. *Jeez . . . I want a cigarette . . . where's the pack? . . . Oh, thanks . . . mm, so good . . .*

The front-seat girl realizes how heavily Fernando's arm is weighing on her now. Gingerly, she tries to shift the pressure. I think they heard us . . . the front-seat girl whispers. No way . . . Fer's snoring . . . The scared girl presses against herself. One of her legs hurts and starts to cramp. She can't move now. She focuses on the cigarettes' little embers and hears the exhalations. Maybe we should get some sleep? . . . says the front-seat girl. Yeah, okay . . . The scared girl stretches out her leg very slowly. The relief is immediate. She closes her eyes; she opens her eyes. The dark is just as dark despite the yellow light of the streetlamps seeping through the curtains and painting a few stripes on the carpet. Cars pass outside. The house is asleep, but the scared girl is wide awake.

She gives Fernando a gentle shake so he'll roll over, and he does, so obediently that he doesn't even wake up or stop storing. The front-seat girl's breath is faint and steady; Rafael's is a mere whistle. Lying on her back, the scared girl thinks of how long she'll have to wait for daybreak and decides to get up before then to use the bathroom and check the time. The others are still the problem. She doesn't want to wake anyone. If she waits a bit, she calculates, they'll all be fast asleep. She stretches out her body as far as she can and closes her eyes again.

When she opens them, there's more light in the living room. She pulls back the blanket and rises to her feet with great caution. She tiptoes over the carpet and goes first to the kitchen for a glance at the clock. There she finds the other girl leaning against the refrigerator, drinking a glass of water. *Hi*, she says. The other girl's cheeks are pink and her smile is crooked when she lowers the glass to receive the scared girl's greeting. *What's up … ? Have you been awake for a while?* The other girl sets the glass into the drying rack without rinsing it and yawns.

What? . . . No . . . I just woke up . . . Toño's in the bathroom . . . What time is it? the scared girl asks. *Five thirty, I think . . . So how was it . . . Oh, amazing . . . and now I'm definitely not a virgin . . . Wow, really? . . . And what's it like, does it hurt a lot? . . . A little, but not as much as they say, it feels scratchy at first, then kind of weird until it's over . . . You'll see . . . Who knows . . . they say it's better the second time . . . Well, I've done it three times and not really . . . Three, wow . . . What about you?* The scared girl doesn't want to tell her that she heard the front-seat girl with Rafael and that she herself was with Fernando and nothing happened to her at all. *Rafael tried to kiss me, but he's an asshole . . . He already tried to get with Rosa and that didn't work either . . . not cool . . . Yeah, no,* the other girl says.

Toño comes in and smiles at them both. He's better-looking in the morning than at night, the scared girl thinks. What's up, girls . . . Nothing much . . . Toño puts his arms around the other girl and gives her a kiss. I'm starving . . . Shhh! The parents are going to hear! The other girl claps her hand over his mouth and Toño wriggles away and kisses her again and the other girl laughs and Toño tickles her and the other girl crumples and throws herself to the ground. The scared girl laughs as if she were part of their game and edges toward the kitchen door. I'm going to the bathroom, she says, but nobody is paying attention.

Back in the living room, she sees Rosa and Rafael

still asleep on the floor, swaddled in their blankets. She walks toward the couch, sits on the edge, and whispers to Fernando: Wake up, it's almost six . . . Fernando opens his eyes, smiles tenderly at her, opens his arms. C'mere . . . The scared girl shrinks back. No . . . careful . . . Rosa's parents get up really early . . . But it's Sunday . . . It doesn't matter . . . You guys have to go, they're going to catch us . . . And the scared girl stands up and steps over to Rosa and nudges her with her foot, Hey . . . wake up . . . come on . . . it's time.

They all sit down together in the kitchen. They smoke quickly as they shuffle through their options. Fernando takes a seat beside the scared girl and strokes her back. Rafael looks nervous and barely glances up from the floor. I'm starving, the other girl says. Let's go, then, says Toño. Rosa smokes one cigarette after another and looks at Rafael, trying to get him to look back. You guys go ahead . . . we'll catch up with you later . . . She walks out of the kitchen and the others fall silent even though Rafael lifts his eyes and looks at Toño and signals to him with his hand. Let's get out of here, man . . . I have to go home . . . I told my mom I'd be back . . . And they file out very quietly and the other girl and the scared girl stand in the hall and Rosa yells from the bathroom: Are they gone? Shhhh . . . be quiet . . . your parents will hear you, says the other. Who cares . . .

They eat some bananas and the other girl suggests

they take a bike ride. But it's only seven in the morning, the scared girl complains. So what, says Rosa in a flash of anger. What's it to you if you . . . I mean, you actually slept, right? . . . or didn't you . . . The scared girl doesn't answer and Rosa walks toward the front hall, where the bikes are. I'll take my dad's, Rosa says, and the other girl and the scared girl mount the brother's bike and the mom's bike. They open the front door. The street is deserted, still muted with shadow; the cool, dry air barely rustles the branches where the birds have started to stir. The sound of the bike treads on the sidewalks' downward slope feels like it was just invented. For a minute, the scared girl feels safe, intensely happy, in possession of a new experience; she stops as Rosa and the other girl pedal off in earnest down the street. What are you doing, hurry up, they shout. And the scared girl places her feet on the pedals and slowly starts to pick up speed until she reaches Rosa and the other girl at the end of the first block, where she looks both ways to make sure no cars are coming and darts ahead, quick as an arrow, on her green bike.

THE DECISION WASN'T MADE BY THE SCARED GIRL BUT BY HER WILL, DEEPER INSIDE

She returned home around 1:00 PM that Sunday. She took a shower and got into bed to read. She fell asleep several times, but the feeling of the light always probed her awake. Her parents called her downstairs around four for some food. *You look tired . . . did you have fun? . . . Yeah, it was okay . . .* She went back to bed afterward and kept reading her novel until after dark, when the sound of the TV distracted her and she got up to watch a movie with her siblings.

At school on Monday, meeting her girlfriends in the usual place, she felt a string snap in her heart. Something had happened inside her persona, though not in her consciousness, and she couldn't understand it any better than she could explain the sudden onset of a headache or muscle pain. Rosa asked What's the matter several times and the other girl examined her through a veil of cigarette smoke and smiled without a word. I'm tired . . . I'll be right back . . . And she left to walk around the soccer field, which was empty at that hour. She walked several laps around a tract of turf, thinking I'll get over it soon, watching how the blades righted themselves slowly after every footstep. She was making her way toward the building when the bell rang to mark the end of recess. Her friends watched her intently, and the other girl exclaimed Come on, they're going to close the doors. She heard the words uttered in a time that no longer included her. Passing the other girl, she gave her a soft little pat on the shoulder to make sure her feelings weren't the same as the sensations fluttering around in her like unwelcome tenants, starting to unpack their bags and occupy the entire house.

What's this "myself" business, she wondered mockingly as she took out her notebook for class. And she tried to examine herself from the inside as the teacher explained the details of the biology experiment they'd be doing that week. What do I see when I see myself. But it was impossible to control the contents. She opened her notebook, took down the date, and started writing. At the end of class, she left without speaking to her friends and made her way to her locker at a near jog.

She slowly grasped the decision her will had made: to isolate herself, to distance herself from people, especially her friends. To avoid, as rigorously as possible, any experience that wasn't essential. Which is to say, solitary. The severity of the decision was so clean, so forceful, that the scared girl became a fanatic of her own cause. She no longer cared if she was rude to her friends, if she greeted them coldly when they approached, if she fled so they'd have no chance to ask What's up, or something even worse. She didn't care if they looked at her like she was crazy, if even her parents said *What on earth is the matter with you, why are you acting so strangely*. All she wanted was to be alone: immersed in her inner life, where nothing was happening yet.

During recess, she'd sometimes go to the library to read or think: staring out the window, listening to the voices that reached her from beyond the glass. She had to fill herself with something, because she was empty. Mystically, the scared girl invented a place in her head. She would be the one giving orders there; she would stand at attention to direct every instant of this new phase. Inside, few faces resisted her discipline. Only I can live here, the scared girl would say to herself, erasing clues; only I will get to know itself or to know me. And she felt the heat inside this place, and she felt sad for people and a glimmer in the shadows that asked her: what's the point of all this? The scared girl knew there wasn't any, and such knowledge allowed her to perceive her depth. How far do I go, and what for, and her eyes filled with tears. She tore a page from her notebook and wrote:

Me and you and you and me
Who are we
Why did we come into the world
What is the world
Questions and more questions

She stuffed the loose sheet into the pages of her notebook and got up to rummage around the shelves. The literature teacher had asked them to read *Demian* by Hermann Hesse, so she looked for it; there it was, beside other books by the same writer, *Siddhartha* and *Steppenwolf.* She sat back down with *Demian* in hand. She rested her head on her arm and closed her eyes until the bell rang.

IT HAPPENED TO *I*, NOT TO ME

She started *Demian* that same afternoon, on the terrace, where the cats arranged themselves on the tiles like blotches of shadow. They stared at her and licked their paws and cleaned their faces and stretched out and slept; sometimes the scared girl stopped reading to watch them and then to seek the horizon beyond the black stripe of the railing and to think again of herself and her life that had barely begun.

Demian wasn't the main character in the novel. Emil Sinclair was, a ten-year-old schoolboy from a good family, disturbed by the double reality of his world: the reality of day and his house, beautiful, orderly, happy clean; the reality of night and the street, dirty, chaotic, teeming with grim faces, disturbances, commotion. Sinclair's existence was divided, mournfully and vicariously, between the two. Sometimes Sinclair would defy his parents and run off into the bustling streets with his friends, fight with his sisters, and sink into moods dark enough to make him feel superior to normal life, where everything happened on time. Sometimes, though, he'd happily coexist with every member of his household. One afternoon, as a result of his own lies, he encountered the first miniature version of the devil: Franz Kromer, a poor and precocious boy who knew the streets, lived without privilege, and attended a public school. Sinclair boasted to him of a made-up feat: he claimed he'd stolen apples from an orchard. Hearing this, Kromer demanded he swear on all he held sacred that his account was true, and Sinclair agreed. The next day, Kromer sought him out and informed him that there was a reward for information on the apple thief. Unless Sinclair was willing to cough up some cash, Kromer intended to give him away and accept the bounty.

So began Sinclair's plight. To assuage the threats, he started paying Kromer the scattered coins he managed to steal from his parents or extract from his piggy bank, but they were never enough. Then a miracle occurred. A new student appeared in the classroom, Max Demian, whose mere presence captured Sinclair's attention. He wasn't like the other boys; he was more serious, more focused, more remote. After class, Demian approached Sinclair and they walked home together. They talked about Cain and Abel, the topic of the day's lesson, and Demian surprised him with an explanation of Cain as a chosen being: "Brave, strong-willed people always seem sinister to the others." He added that the mark of Cain was a privilege, a sign of power and clarity. Sinclair's strict religious education prevented him from agreeing. But he couldn't stop thinking about the mark, and he even thought he caught a glimpse of it on Demian's forehead. Little by little, after several walks, Sinclair started telling Demian about his terrible dilemma with Kromer. Without ever revealing how, Demian made sure that Kromer would never bother him again. And Sinclair resumed his luminous life, though burdened now with new knowledge: "I realize today that nothing in the world is more distasteful to a man than to take the path that leads to himself."

The scared girl closed the book and looked up raptly at the ceiling. She touched her forehead. The mark was there, she was sure of it: *It's the sign of my* I, she told herself. To get to know it better, she'd have to sequester herself away; inside was a receptacle, a chamber, a room. *I* peered in alongside the scared girl. She could still hear the chatter of the outside world. Like sparklers, ringing the air and crackling with light. *If it's really* I, *then I have to go deeper in.* The room was as large as *I*'s consciousness and there were no ghosts in the brownish-gray walls. *They used to be white*, a new voice said to the scared girl, and she knew it was *I*. To keep the center of *I*'s perception from dissolving, the scared girl had to control her every act and every thought. And to hold on to the notion of the room—because as soon as she lost track of it, her head filled with simultaneous presences, memories, anticipations, trifling interferences like *now I'm getting up and going to the kitchen, No, first I'll pet this cat, No, I've got to scratch this itch, No, I'd better wait, No, I should really go to the kitchen and get a glass of water or something to distract myself or distract time . . .*

And so the scared girl's mind trotted on when *I* failed to take the reins. Just like that, scurrying right along beside herself, the girl she once was, which was the obstacle: the fourteen years she'd already lived without *I*.

At school, the scared girl and *I* devised a way to spend recess. Instead of wandering around the official area designated for the smokers and the high school kids, where her girlfriends invariably were, they'd head for the field in front of the elementary school. There they'd sit with their backs against a tree and read. *I* was still stiff, like a pale cardboard sheet barely crinkled with lines or folds. The scared girl knew she had to shed her fear so that *I* would at least have the chance to manifest itself. But she'd have to file down some rough edges first.

There had to be rules, the scared girl resolved.

Destroying her vanity was the most important one. She stopped looking at herself in the mirror and primping, and she adopted an austere style of dress: brown pants or blue jeans, a loose blouse, nearly military-style boots. She wore her hair in a perpetual ponytail. No earrings or makeup. Nothing with any ties to her prior persona. Maybe this way *I* could bloom.

It was dangerous, this introspective journey. "One must be capable of entering oneself entirely, like a turtle," Demian told Sinclair. But where is one exactly? The scared girl tried to concentrate on the room where *I* reigned, then shifted her gaze to the grass, pulled up a blade, and tickled herself on the arm with the tip. She found it strange to have skin. Skin covered up the *I* and made it impossible to converse with it unmediated, condemned it to existing inside while she hovered outside, desperate, because the entrance was very narrow. The scared girl lingered around this sensation for a few minutes, trying to slip in through a crack, but it wouldn't stay still. Reading calmed her down.

Summer break and a new school meant that Sinclair and Demian grew apart. Life changed abruptly and Sinclair started spending his nights in bars, drinking uncontrollably. Demian was a hollow in his soul and he had to fill it with alcohol. Sinclair made his way home near dawn every night, blind drunk. "Losing yourself is a sin," Demian had told him . . .

The scared girl remembered a memory: in her bedroom one night, she heard shouts outside her window. A drunk couple, the woman far drunker than the man, was fighting on the sidewalk in front of the house. The woman was sprawled out on the ground and the man was yelling Get up, goddammit, get up already, you fucking bitch, and she wailed Leave me here, just leave me alone for God's sake. The scared girl felt a rush of vertigo and pressed her hands over her ears. The drama went on for ten more minutes. At last, the scared girl got into bed, burrowing deep under the covers. Life shouldn't be like this, she said to herself, on the verge of tears, still unsheltered by *I*, her inner cables in disarray, tangled and knotted as erratically as the tentacles of a trapped animal.

Now she felt protected. Awkward as it was, *I* was pure and transparent. Silence helped her see more clearly. The trouble was the scared girl's inevitable experience, the difficulty of being *I* in the everyday space of school and home that jeopardized the inward slope where the scared girl could slip down into another origin. Not this one, not here.

SHE MUST GO FOR *I* TO COME

The scared girl wasn't sure if she'd decided to feel special or if she'd discovered that she actually was, and so she resolved to play the part. In any case, with her attire, her isolation, and her quiet discipline, she had already assumed the role in everyone else's eyes, even though *I*, inside, remained an unfinished project, and she had to summon it deliberately; its presence didn't automatically manifest itself. Her fourteen-year-old life carried on its backward and forward path as if nothing had changed. The spiritual parallels with Sinclair and Demian were growing clearer, though they weren't unobstructed. The most obvious hurdle was womanhood. The scared girl decided to erase any signs that pointed toward the conclusion "*I* is she." No: it was *I*. She would ignore sex so intensely that it would vanish altogether and the scared girl could subsist in a state of perennial childhood or preadolescence. If she was to get rid of her face, she couldn't look at herself in the mirror anymore. That way, when she examined herself from within, she wouldn't have a physical identity and *I* would flourish in limbo.

The other two obstacles—the place, Mexico City; the time, the 1970s—were no less significant. The scared girl hadn't yet come up with a way to disrupt the external evidence. For now, all she could do was mostly ignore it. Sometimes she managed to distort the notion of time; it's the mind, after all, that filters time and can deform it. Sinclair and Demian were teenagers in Germany before World War I. But they lived in neighborhoods, not on the grand stages of History. A neighborhood is any old neighborhood, and Coyoacán, the scared girl's neighborhood, had old, ruinous features—"European" features, as it were—that encouraged the fallacy. The scared girl circumscribed her walks: down Francisco Sosa to the little Aguacate alleyway, then several loops around the Santa Catarina plaza, then back up Francisco Sosa to Tres Cruces and the Plaza Centenario. She always looked down at the ground and never at the passersby, her hands clasped behind her back, her head full of instructions. If they don't see you and you don't see them, she doesn't exist, the scared girl would say to herself, walking at a fast clip. Haste was another feature of discipline. It's impossible to think if you're slow. Or impossible to think well.

The scared girl practiced her metamorphosis by walking. Walking, she could plan her future. When everything functioned automatically at last, when *I* had become her nature, not her script, spontaneity would return. Meanwhile, she had to guide her inner life blindly, omitting any desires of her own. Her mind brooded alone with the scared girl's persona and without *I*: it was she and it never left. Like a logical flaw that unravels any outcome unless it's corrected before the end of the movie. What movie, though, if there was still no story to be told? That Sinclair was a fragile, sensitive soul and Demian a kind of demiurge wasn't enough information to solve the problem of the scared girl and *I*. What would become of them?

To spur the transformation, or at least create a void, the scared girl adopted an exercise invented by Sinclair in the absence of his friend Demian: she sat up very straight in a hard-backed chair, fixed her eyes on a single point, and stayed perfectly still until she couldn't take it anymore. She did this every night before bed. The goal was to control the contents of her head and punish anything that strayed from the proper course, which something always did; at the slightest opportunity, the scared girl found herself drifting along the narrow paths of pleasure, of intimacy, where it was easy to get comfortable and remember or anticipate. Then she had to slam on the brakes, clear out the room in her head, and repeat again: I'm *I*, not her. She sat even straighter until her back hurt a little. Then she got into bed to keep reading. Books had become manuals. After Demian, she'd leapt to Nietzsche because of a confession of Sinclair's: "During those weeks I had begun to read a book that made a more lasting impression on me than anything I had read before. Even later in life I have rarely experienced a book more intensely, except perhaps Nietzsche." The author of the book in question was Novalis. The scared girl looked for it among her father's books, but all she found was a volume of Nietzsche. She showed it to her father, who explained, "*Thus Spoke Zarathustra*! I took that book with me when I went to Barra Navidad. But be careful; I wound up crazy, talking with the ocean." The scared girl had no time to hear the story all over again. Her dad's excitement strengthened her resolve, but she didn't want to get her anecdotes confused or find herself burdened with any interpretation that might pollute her own. "Yeah, you told me already," she said, and smiled before retreating to her room. Her parents must have been worried about the scared girl: she didn't go out with her friends anymore, she dressed like a boy, she barely spoke, she read all the time. Although their worry was probably tinged with pride. Their daughter was odd, no doubt about it, but she read a lot, which some parents find reassuring. The scared girl observed them indulgently: Poor things, they're hopeless, she said to herself. The situation with her siblings was more complicated. They mocked her: "Ha, ha! Here comes the butch! Want to borrow my work boots? Ha, ha!" The scared girl felt little stabs of indignation, but she didn't answer. Inside was *I* and they, her siblings, couldn't possibly imagine the dimensions of the space. She locked herself in her room and thought about how she'd surprise everyone someday, when inside and outside fit together like two identical pieces.

WITH *I* ON THE ROOF

Her dad had built a tiny one-room studio on the roof in hopes of seeking refuge to paint and listen to music, but his life was short on free time and the room—complete with bathroom, bed, drafting table, bench, and two chairs—remained unoccupied. The scared girl asked permission to use it in the afternoons. She'd settle onto the bench at the drafting table and write in her notebook:

> Zarathustra "left his home and the lake of his home" when he was thirty. He went into the mountains. I'm in mine. My mountain is this room. Here I have to learn how to be *I*.

Sometimes one of the cats would stop by to visit, jump up onto the table, settle onto the notebook, lick one paw and then the other. The scared girl would wait patiently for the cat to get bored of being bored and relocate to the bed. It would always look into her eyes before it decamped. When the scared girl tired of writing or reading, she'd carefully lie down next to the cat. *Cats are my spirits. They watch over me.* The scared girl would review her day with *I*'s newfound awareness, but the ordinary voice of her head usually got in the way, interjecting sheer nonsense: Memo, the good-looking boy who distracted her from her notes; so-and-so's outfit;

her friends smoking in the distance as she made a bee-line for her tree. The scared girl wasn't sure if she could switch off her inner machine. She focused on Sinclair and Demian, who had run into each other on the street by chance after years without seeing each other, and they'd resumed their usual conversation, their usual silence. Sinclair had stopped drinking; he was a studious young man who drew and had recurring dreams, especially one about a bird with enormous wings. The scared girl generally couldn't remember her dreams, but she resolved to pay more attention to her nights. She also bought a sketchbook and set down her first lines with a paintbrush and some India ink she'd asked her father for. Her drawings were abstract, although she sometimes glimpsed a face in profile amid the streaks and splotches. Once she even tried to draw Sinclair's bird, but the childishness of her rendition sent her straight back into another spell of intense reading. Her ruminations yielded at least one certainty: her forehead bore the mark. She could feel it with her fingers, a sensitive spot between her eyebrows, a hidden hollow, an incipient stripe. Sinclair, Demian, and *I* belonged to the same sect of chosen beings. Although the scared girl would have struggled to describe each step, she knew that the transformation had already occurred, or at least the first part: *I* had taken the lead. When this triumph began to dissipate, the scared girl would reread the last line of

Demian: " . . . I need only bend over that dark mirror to behold my own image, now completely resembling him, my brother, my master."

This lesson, this prayer, was the incentive in the scared girl's mind. If she lost her way, she'd invoke the brother, the master, the dark mirror. She'd press her eyelids shut and clench her teeth and her fists, and in this rigidity, standing bolt upright in the rooftop room, she'd feel a rush of purity. Then she'd return to the drafting table and write in her notebook: "Today I saw the vision in the black mirror. I finally saw myself as I'm going to be." And she'd pick up her Nietzsche again so that the scene she'd just captured in her mind wouldn't budge. She'd underline the parts she didn't want to forget: "It is the hour of great contempt," Zarathustra proclaimed before a crowd that mocked him. He'd stayed in the mountains for ten years, immersed in contemplation until he had grown "weary of [his] wisdom, like the bee that hath gathered too much honey." And so he'd decided to go down into the neighboring village to share his knowledge. He quickly ran into an old man who recognized him: "Altered is Zarathustra; a child hath Zarathustra become; an awakened one is Zarathustra: what wilt thou do in the land of the sleepers?" Zarathustra explained to him that he loved mankind and had come bearing a gift. The old man replied that only God mattered and men were far too imperfect. Zarathustra walked away, murmuring, "This old saint in the forest hath not yet heard of it, that GOD IS DEAD!"

Zarathustra believed that the spirit had to undergo three metamorphoses: into a camel, into a lion, and into a child. The camel carries, the lion tries to attain freedom, and the child plays. The lion says *I want* where the camel had said *I must*, but he doesn't know how to forge new values and he lacks the gift of negligence: "Innocence is the child, and forgetfulness, a new beginning, a game, a self-rolling wheel, a first movement, a holy Yea . . . for the game of creating, my brethren, there is needed a holy Yea until life . . ." The scared girl was perplexed by the equation. Her plan was solemnity, and now she'd stumbled into the formula for play. In another part of the book, she read a line that threatened her project: "I hate the reading idlers." For an instant, she felt the presence of her guilt like a passive, invasive body. But Zarathustra reviled reading and passivity after spending so long in his mountain refuge, and the scared girl had barely dipped a toe into her own solitude. She'd have to be brave if she was to overcome the impending trials. She realized that it wouldn't be enough to simply spend her afternoons hanging out on the roof; she'd have to prolong and sharpen her seclusion, spend hours and hours up there with her thoughts and her flimsy spirit, reading as the contents cascaded over her in disarray, flocking back to her like small, realistic creatures.

The scared girl communicated to her parents that she'd decided to start sleeping in the rooftop room as well. They looked at her and shrugged: "Well . . . if that's what you want . . ." Her mother went upstairs for an inspection: "It's filthy . . . You'll have to wait for me to clean it first." Two days later, it was ready, gleaming; the bed was made, the bathroom stocked with towels and toilet paper. That afternoon the scared girl stayed downstairs, watching TV. She had to be serene, fully prepared for her first night alone.

It was an overseen sleep, a staging. The scared girl slept and observed herself sleeping. At dawn, she sat down at the drafting table and listed various details of her new adventure in her notebook:

1. Noises on the roof, like rustling branches, quiet footsteps, creaks.
2. A cat scratched at the door, meowing.
3. I dreamed of Mom. We were walking down the street, holding hands, and the road was full of puddles and we couldn't cross it.
4. I woke up lots of times. Sleeping upstairs thins out the night, sharpens its blade.
5. I have to hang in there.

She showered quickly, went down for breakfast, and climbed into the car with her siblings. She said nothing on the way to school. She felt proud of her secret life and confident that nothing would distract her from it ever again. "Flee, my friend, into thy solitude!" She repeated Nietzsche's words in her head like a prayer. Now I'm finally going to be *I*, the scared girl said to herself. Sitting under her tree at recess, she felt a glimmer of the lucidity that would surely consume her as soon as she'd managed to eradicate all traces of her previous persona. She imagined everything she was going to think, the depths of the abyss, the words she'd hear in her head. She'd have to domesticate her feelings and avoid sadness, even if she did find it more complex than happiness. The camel was sad, not the lion or the child. "I should only believe in a God that would know how to dance," Zarathustra declared. "And when I saw my devil, I found him serious, thorough, profound, solemn."

The scared girl discovered that music was the perfect guide for her inner experience. Some afternoons, before dinner and before she went up to the roof for the night, she'd put on one of her father's records, lying down on the living room couch and listening to a symphony or a quartet with tears in her eyes. I'm almost there, *I* whispered to her. And one day or one night, upstairs or downstairs, the scared girl saw a small gray door: she opened it and stepped in, first one foot, then the other, then her whole body, then her face, her hands feeling their way along the surface of the air. There was nothing inside the space, but it was all *I*. The scared girl faded away until she was gone.

I

I'm going to think of words.

I'm going to think of colors.

I'm going to think of noises.

I'm going to think of the world.

I'm going to think of nothingness.

I'm going to think of God.

I'm going to think of smells.

I'm going to think of death.

I'm going to think of bells.

I'm going to think of adult conversations.

I'm going to think of political arguments.

I'm going to think.

I learned it in a book.

It's a green book.

It's a book called *Portrait of the Artist as a Young Man*.

It's a book by James Joyce.

It's a book that tells the story of Stephen Dedalus.

It's a book that starts like this:

Once upon a time and a very good time it was there was a moocow coming down along the road and this moocow that was down along the road met a nicens little boy named baby tuckoo . . .

It's me!

I keep reading. There's an argument between
his parents and relatives and a friend. The
boy listens from a corner at the table and gets
upset because their voices rise and his father
weeps. Words are things in his head and also
in mine. I listen to my parents as we eat. What
they're saying tells another story when it mixes
with me. "Like something in a book," says
Dedalus. And me too and I focus on the sun-
beams angling through the window, scattering
across the table that's a marble slab mounted
on a concrete base, my dad made it when we
lost the other house and we moved to this little
place above the restaurant. My parents fight a
lot although my dad never cries like Dedalus's
dad but he does yell and my mom gets quiet
looking down at her hands and I want her to
talk back but she never does. Every word leads
to another word and another experience in
Dedalus's head: *Suck was a queer word*. And
Dedalus remembers how once he was with his
dad in a hotel and after washing his hands his
dad lifted the plug from the sink and the water
made that sucking noise, louder when it went
down the tubes. I wish I could remember like
Dedalus but I've never been to a hotel, I've
only been in houses. Water doesn't make that

noise in my house. But there are other things
that have the same rhythm and I recite them
to myself as they happen: the thread of water
on the terrace where I read gets thinner when
it reaches the gap in the railing and spreads
with its bubbles, I try to imagine what Dedalus
would have said, that the water was cold, not
hot, and it was very odd that faucets had letters on them, but suddenly he was in school
listening to his teacher and I'm on my way to
mine every morning, trapped in the car with
my siblings and my mom at the wheel, I cover
my face with my notebook so no one pays any
attention to whether I'm a girl or a boy because
I'm the voice from inside and that's what the
voice sounds like and it has no face or it's the
face of Stephen Dedalus and when I get to
school I walk close to the wall in the corridors,
wearing my brown corduroy pants, my boots,
my boy's shirt, my ponytail, and I hide in the
library to read during recess and I don't go to
my tree anymore because if I run into any of
the elementary school kids they point at me
and laugh and I'm not used to being made fun
of although I know it doesn't matter because I
have a secret life and they don't and they don't
get that my face isn't my real face because I'm

building it and one day my thoughts will be visible there and I'll walk around in peace again.
Now it's just at home, in my room on the roof,
with a cat or two, sitting at the drafting table
or lying in bed, that I manage to make my way
down the slope that takes me to Dedalus and
it's a narrow place, always twilight, where I
settle in and go back over the mistake of living where I live and I touch my cheek because
he touches his and it feels cold under his fingers and he thinks it must be white and he
wonders if all white things are cold and damp
and he thinks of other colors and red roses and
a green place where maybe green roses grow
and the vertigo I feel as I go down the slope is
so intense that I close my eyes and other colors bloom that can also be thought of, yellow,
blue, purple, gray, and I try but nothing occurs
to me, so I keep reading, Dedalus is away at
boarding school, he observes his classmates,
he finds them strange, as I find mine, and my
friends from before keep staring as if they
knew me and sometimes one of them comes
up to me in the hall to talk and I just say yes
or no and walk away quickly and Dedalus gets
sick but it's because of sadness: *He thought he
was sick in his heart if you could be sick in that*

place. And one day in literature class a new
kid asked another if I was a girl or a boy and
they both laughed and they looked at me and
I hid my enormous feet under the table and
pretended I hadn't heard, it's not easy wandering around the world with your face dislocated, unable to look at yourself in the mirror,
because Dedalus gets lost, it's a rule, it would
mean betraying him, *Don't go*, I shout to him,
it's already happened before that I can't find
him, so I return to the book where the noises
take me by the hand, impose their distance and
alter it as I cover and uncover my ears, noises
that come from far away and show up late,
other very nearby ones that belong to wherever you're sitting or lying down, noises from
a machine, from the cars outside, or closer
still, like the voices of my mom or my siblings,
sometimes I lose hope because I can't make it
permanent, my life on the slope with Dedalus,
I hit my head with my fists and cry and the
cat or cats look at me startled and dart out of
the room and don't come back, no matter how
much I call to them, and I go back to the book,
alone now, Dedalus is studying geography, trying to memorize the names of all the countries
in the Americas but he can't, different places

with different names: *They were all in different countries and the countries were in continents and the continents were in the world and the world was in the universe.*

And in my diary I take notes like him:

I

In my room
In my house
In my neighborhood
In my city
In my country
In my continent
In the world
In the universe

What comes after the universe? Nothing. And after that: god. No one has ever seen noth-ingness, some have seen god, I haven't, even though sometimes I sneak into church, pen-itent because I wasn't baptized, and my dad says he's the devil, that if he enters a church smoke wafts up from his every footstep, and he laughs and everyone else laughs with him, but I don't because god and Dedalus coex-ist in the same place and god has no name but god and I don't have a name anymore but I will

soon when I don't have to leave the slope anymore. The smoke from his footsteps smells
like sulfur, says my dad, and my mom looks at
him smiling, almost relieved, finally he's not
in a bad mood anymore, *Ay, Jaime*, they burst
out laughing again, and I'd like to tell them
that god isn't a game, that the devil doesn't
smell like anything, that's why he can trick
you, that god smells like rain, though, like wet
dust, like the narrow cobblestone street I walk
along some afternoons with the stones pol-
ished by the water, my boots slip on them and
the mud smells like crushed grass and dirt
and pebbles, like the countryside, that's it, a
meadow, a clean smell, innocent, air brush-
ing against the ground, the arched spine of my
favorite cat, gray with white patches, purity,
silk, although Dedalus thinks of different
smells, the farmers' campfire, corduroy drying by the hearth, his life has more details than
mine does, but I'm just getting started, yesterday I read the part about the fire, Dedalus
lying in bed and watching the winter sun on
the glass, *He wondered if he would die*, you can
die at any moment, even on a beautiful day,
with a perfect summery sun, people happy in
the street, walking, chatting, kids playing ball

or chasing each other, you can die out of the
blue, because the fever rises and no one pays
attention, everyone's distracted outside, and
I'm lying in bed in my rooftop room, getting
worse and worse, delirious, watching night-
mares on the walls, thinking about how sad it
will be if I die, how they'll have to change my
clothes, make me up for the coffin, will they
put me in my brown pants and my boots or a
dress and a little girl's pointy black shoes? My
friends will come, they'll say what a tragedy,
she looks so pretty, they'll cry and my mom
will kneel down beside me, covering her face
in her hands, sobbing, and my siblings will also
cry and they'll all think about how they left me
alone so they could go out and play, so they'll
never forget me because they'll feel guilty forever and my siblings will feel even worse for
making fun of me so much, but my death will
bring them together, they'll remember me
at breakfast and in the car on the way to the
school and they'll shut the door of the rooftop room without touching a thing, it'll be a
sacred place, and sometimes my mom will go
up to clean and she'll open my notebook and
read my notes, but she won't understand anything because they're written in code, it's hard

to know who's who, me or Dedalus, like when the bells ring, is it him listening or me? They sound ancient from my room and then I can make my way down the slope, *dingdong, dingdong*, until I find myself in Dedalus, Dublin, along the Liffey, roiling river, a horse clops by, pulling a wagon, the gravel crunches on the path, I slip a hand into my pocket, there's a coin, I finger it, Dedalus, what a strange name, what a strange boy, *Are you good at riddles?* I'm not, I mix up words in my panic, I root around in my head like a dog in pursuit of a missing bone, *dedal* means thimble in Spanish, thimbles, labyrinth, Stephen, Esteban, *estaban* means *they were*, let me be *I* without my face on the slope, going where, come here, this way, this is the house of a writer and a painter, my grandmother lives in it, a tiny two-story house, my grandmother lives upstairs in bed, sighing or reading or drowsing, I admire her long, white, bony hands, *Tower of Ivory, House of Gold. By thinking of things you could understand them*, my grandmother touches her cool fingers to my face when I lean in to give her a kiss on the cheek, my mom sits with her, they both look at me and smile, I go downstairs to the living room, I settle myself onto the warm, soft

rug in front of the fireplace with no wood in it,
I contemplate the hollow chimney, it hints at
winter, concave Dublin, the river is the wind,
my grandmother's voice upstairs has the foreign murmur of history, of another century, my
mom answers her in daughterspeak, and I roll
down the slope that opens out like a simple,
generous slide, I slide smoothly down, I stay
still for a few moments, *The noise of children at
play annoyed him and their silly voices made him
feel . . . that he was different from others. He did
not want to play. He wanted to meet in the real
World the unsubstantial image which his soul so
constantly beheld*, I get distracted, what are they
talking about, it doesn't matter, says my dad
or Dedalus's dad, they killed him, they killed
our hero or took him prisoner or disappeared
him, our hero, *who*, the slope shifts, starts to
fade away, *don't let go of the voices, stay there*,
but I can't do it anymore, I come up from the
slope, return to the living room, grab a cushion, slam it into the rug, I AM NOT *I*, hurling
the cushion across the room, there used to be
a door, now there's nothing to open or close.
How to get out? How to get in? And one day I
touch myself between my legs and the next day
I punish myself, torture my senses, although

skin isn't a sense, but who cares, I hurt it a
little, I scratch it, I pinch it, then my ears, I
make a shrill noise with a wire on a metal edge
or constantly clear my throat or shriek like a
monkey to annoy myself, and for my sense of
smell I sniff cat poop or pee, the dry residue
of egg in the pan, my dirty hair, and for taste
I lick dirt, eat soap, my dad's fish dinner, salt
on the tongue until it burns, and at night I lie
down crooked in bed, on wrinkled sheets so
the creases bother me and if my leg cramps
up I stay still until I feel purified by pain and
Dedalus also tortures himself and when I get a
ride to school, hiding my face behind my notebook, I think of everything I've learned and
how easily I could lose it if I accepted the outside rules, but I'm here, I have no mercy on
myself, the slope opens with the pain, it closes
with indulgence, at school I'm a shadow, at
home, in my room, Dedalus consoles me with
the *rhythms of beauty*, the voices inside, at last,
the boy's coming, he erases me, the order is
like a ticket to somewhere else, *Away then: it is
time to go. A voice spoke softly to Stephen's lonely
heart, bidding him go*, and one night I wake up
shouting, gasping for air, my heart, my heart,
and I run from the room, dash down the stairs,

and my mom hugs me and my dad gives me
a pill and I stay with them and I don't go up
to the room anymore and Dedalus calls to me
and I call to myself and I don't have a face anymore, for him or for me, and I watch TV every
afternoon to keep from thinking and one day I
gather my nerve to look at myself in the mirror,
I lock myself in the bathroom and step closer
to the mirror and stand in front of myself and
say it's her but the image in the mirror doesn't
recognize me and I hide again, dead or who
knows how far she'll go, who will I be tomorrow, tell me, please, sweet girl, sweet boy.

4.

FATHER, MOTHER, CHILDREN

The meeting place is a photograph. My parents and sister and I are posing in the living room of our first house. My father's right hand rests on the shoulder of my sister, who sits on a stool in front of him. My mother holds me in her lap. All four of us are smiling, looking at the camera. Behind us is a brick wall with two framed paintings. My father's body is thrust forward in an expectant stance. The look on his face suggests a certain impatience, as if he were reluctant to be there, as if he'd been interrupted on his way to something else. It's the photo of his family thus far (two more children would follow), and also the beginning of a story—or, better put, of the scraps of a story.

Maybe there are no happy families, just happy days. I remember them because they're always flanked by unhappy ones. The day the photo was taken might have been one of those, despite my father's intentions; his temperament often ruptured the natural course of things. The photo session must have irritated him. He didn't believe in commemorations, much less my mother's feelings, which he usually dismissed as silly or naive. "Come on, Jaime, it'll be quick," my mother would have insisted, and he would have barked, "What a hassle, Joan, but fine, fine, let's get it over with," before sitting in front of the camera for a few minutes. Afterward, I'm sure he'd have gone right back to his studio: a loft above the living room with a railing he could lean on to survey the entire space. There, my father had set up his drafting table and architect's instruments for drawing blueprints, measuring spaces, sketching lines. Rolls of paper covered the surface; a plastic container held blue pencils with points of varying thickness. The sense of order was as beautiful as the objects that composed it.

At the time the photo was taken, I didn't yet know any of what I'm describing to you now. My memory of the old house, for example, comes after the framed image adorning my own studio today. Sometimes I dream of that living room and try to reconstruct it when I wake. My father had commissioned all the furniture, except for the rocking chair and another wooden chair or two, to be made with brick. The bases were covered with cushions to form sofas; the coffee table was set onto a rectangular granite slab. Next to the living room was a kind of three-level platform, like a small pyramid; in a hollow at the center were many spheres of clear glass.

Behind the pyramid, at the other end of the room, was a wicker chair facing a heavy old TV set. You could access the dining room along both sides of the pyramid.

Beyond the minor miracle of memory, this reconstruction matters little, although it does speak to the style of an atmosphere. The fact that the furniture was impossible to move also says something about bodies and their tensions. My father was obsessed with comfort and wanted to challenge it by proposing other ways of sitting or lying down. The wicker chair, the rocking chair, and maybe one or two others were concessions to my mother's conventionalism. His ideal scenario was to have us squatting on the floor in homage to some ancestors or other. He believed in reeducating the body's growth toward something practical, more conscious. Years later, his antichair campaign took on the shrillness of a desperate act; he couldn't convince anyone that it was worth sacrificing actual seats for the sake of a cold floor or a rug where your bones would end up digging like splinters into your flesh. He perfected his utopia with foam rubber: in his ideal house, this material would encase walls and floors, making everything a potential chair or bed. The mockup he lugged from office to office displayed the tiny figure of a woman in a bathrobe leaning against a cushioned wall. The model house, or the apartment, really, was shaped like an egg, with enormous glass curves demarcating the oval.

Inside, the foam rubber yellowed the light. There was nothing in it except for the kitchen and bathroom furniture, also products of my father's pessimistic ingenuity. His architecture presupposed an already devastated world, a world of water shortages and overpopulation. Proudly, fervently, he'd declare that there would be no plants or pets in his new world, no wasted energy, no entertainment without a social purpose. We'd all live in these eggs and we'd adapt our habits to a program of monastic rigor and austerity. Compliance would be our sole pleasure.

This, of course, came years after the photo, which was taken at a time when there was still room for wastefulness. My father, architect of unreal structures, ran a restaurant where he focused his efforts to keep the family afloat. In his free time, he painted scenes with revolutionary messages or realist portraits of people who would disappear without coming to collect them. The paintings accumulated in my father's studio without anyone ever daring to ask about the story behind each face. The restaurant brimmed with the zeal for originality that always predisposed my father against ordinary life. The menus were extravagant, the décor eccentric, the waiters even more so. My mother was his dam against excess. She saw to cultivating just enough conservatism to ensure the survival of the restaurant. My father railed violently against her efforts. They'd go for days without speaking, and we had to navigate his dismissive gestures as if they were ghosts or visions fashioned out of too much silence. When peace was restored, their enthusiasm, both my father's and my mother's, felt exaggerated, even feigned, as if rancor was the real dye that colored the atmosphere.

Happiness didn't sit well with my father, but reticence did—or, in extreme cases, rage, which he embraced as a true nature, finally stripped of its disguise. I responded with equal fear to his cheerfulness and his temper. I liked him best when he worked in his studio or in the kitchen, inventing some dish to feed and please us. When I heard his voice nearby, I felt my nerves prickle as if preparing for an attack. It didn't always come, but habit doesn't account for exceptions. Any eventuality was fragile when it came to my father: you could talk with him until the demands, the advice, the orders invariably began. His affection was programmatic and he didn't seem to understand any relationship that lacked a concrete outcome. I learned to slip away or appease him under duress. In my head, though, thoughts scurried like panicked animals as my father's mouth snapped open and shut like a trap. There was an entire period—again, later than the photo—in which my father read Og Mandino and decided that what mattered most in the life of every human being was to sell. For weeks, he assailed us with impassioned speeches on the art of commerce and commanded us to go out and convince people to buy something, anything, from us. Speeches gave way to reproaches: "You bunch of good-for-nothings, you'll never accomplish anything in life. You have to sell, sell, sell." We kids would slink into our corners, our hideouts, waiting for the outburst to subside. On other occasions, our father would riddle us with what he viewed as essential questions: "Who are you? What are you? Where are you going?" And when we stammered in response, he'd come up with another argument to entrap us like clumsy insects seeking only the heat of a light bulb. His taste for it was strange. He liked watching us flounder and would mock us as soon as he saw we'd given up, as if we were his prey and he a hunter of vague and fearful creatures. When he'd seized us in his paws at last, he'd regard us with a love so absolute that it made reciprocity impossible: there was no room for it. I never knew whether that was his goal.

But I keep getting ahead of the photo, where other things are perceptible. The family is a circuit of lightness. I'm a baby; my sister is still a solitary child in her firstborn kingdom. Everything has yet to happen because I've just arrived. It's not my life, it's theirs. My mother's arms encircle me with a sense of wariness; she still hasn't appropriated this baby; I'm barely there. My father wears a smile of struggle. I rarely heard him laugh. His face was not an expressive one; at most, it divulged traces of irritation. In the photo, in that house, or at least at that date, the future was the light that angled into the room, illuminating us as if we contained it. We must have scattered after posing; it was the middle of the day, there were still hours left. My father always had appointments, things to do. I remember him leaving the house with a briefcase to meet with a lawyer who was going to help him with some property mix-up. There were tons of those, a constant trail of shysters, whose primary objective was to con my father and turn a profit without considering the results of whatever dispute we always lost. How else to explain the fact that we were kicked out of every house we lived in? It happened the first time after a trip to the US with my mother. My father stayed behind. On our return, he had already moved us out of the house in the photo to an apartment above the restaurant, where he'd adapted the space with bricks to simulate separate bedrooms. Our belongings were strewn around the tiny makeshift rooms, and my father's studio ended up occupying a corner of the living room, where he set up the drafting table and the objects left after our move. And after our pillage: my siblings and I had been squandering his instruments for the sake of imaginary games, the forts we'd build out of mud and rocks, having first made our own diagrams. Curiously, my father didn't object to this gradual plunder; it was like it gave him an excuse to retreat from architecture. Sitting at his drafting table in the apartment, which lacked even the slightest hope for intimacy, he'd focus on managing the restaurant and on sketching and planning his next projects, which, in his words, would make him famous and us millionaires. Most of these projects involved Mexico City and its inhabitants. My father decided that the only way to save the city was to build it a second story: people would live upstairs, while downstairs would be reserved for cars and parking and public transit. He made spectacular drawings of the new city and the bikes and collective scooters we'd use to travel around the restricted spaces up above. Finishing his plans, he tried to make appointments with city officials to present his idea and win their support. They'd always give him a date and time, and then an hour before the meeting, when my father was getting ready to leave, a secretary would call to cancel. Every time, we'd have to pretend that my father's presence at his drafting table, clearing his throat and shuffling papers, was perfectly normal, although we could tell from his own excitement that at four or five he was going to meet with some man who would ice the cake of our glorious future. By nightfall, my father's resignation had been recycled, and he'd continue bombarding us with propaganda for his city or some other nascent enterprise.

There were many such projects, although two were the most persistent. The first, taking on the magnitude of family myth, involved some land on the coast of Acapulco, the definitive possession of which would have required the army to evict the occupants who'd been living there for years. The deeds were in someone else's hands, but they would be ours if we applied the proper methods. It was such a thorny affair that I learned to distract myself as soon as it came up in conversation. My father was adamant that the property was rightfully ours and he intended to build a chain of hotels on the beach. To do so, all he needed was to appropriate the land and come up with the funds. This land was usually discussed in the evening, as my parents drank their aperitifs before dinner. Their shared euphoria felt more like a wish than a reality. By the third or fourth drink, my mother would start to betray a certain sense of caution, which would gradually tug the conversation toward more neutral territory until dinner was over and it was time for bed.

The second project involved the Spanish language. According to my father, it was full of superfluous letters and sounds. He invented a philology, you might call it— rudimentary, to be sure, but efficient in its interventions. For a time, he immersed himself in the books of Carlos Fuentes, modifying them to obey his new grammar. When he was finished, he asked my mother to deliver the revised books to their author. I think she did, on two or three occasions, without ever receiving the response

he'd always imagined; that is, Fuentes's heartfelt gratitude to my father for having freed him from excess. My
father's language prospered in a strictly personal realm.
What he wrote from then on—notes, descriptions of
his subsequent projects—was composed entirely in this
system, which was somewhere between phonetics and
vowel-suppression. He was an excellent calligraphist,
so the vowels' physical depiction expressed the full
range of their form. The result was illegible, if beautiful enough to pass for a painting. Fortunately, my father
never took the step into oral speech, and so he spared
us the challenge of having to decipher his conversations
in the Spanish he'd altered and reduced. The sound
would have consisted of amassed consonants, no syllables, a nomenclature of peculiar noises. I once heard
him read his texts aloud from the drafting table in our
unwalled apartment. The language lent itself to cartoon
adaptation.

His plans were as constant as their failures. At
night, over drinks, the panorama was promising, but the
whispers from my parents' bedroom the next morning
conveyed distress. In our presence, they acted as if harmony were the norm, as if moving to a new house out
of the blue could be as fun as a carnival where you lost
your identity for several hours. They treated the change
as something that suited us all. But my father's temper
soured, and in the mornings, when it was time for him to

settle accounts at the restaurant, he exuded desperation. Money became a central theme; never again would it be extricated from our daily lives. Discussing money meant not having it, and my father turned his obsessive attention to the lives of businessmen, like a devotee longing to emulate the saints. At meals, he'd recite the feats of men who had started out selling neckties downtown and were now the owners of textile emporia. He urged his children to follow in their footsteps. We'd stare at him, perplexed, never knowing whether the conversation would end in wrath or silence. We all had our own special method for coping with his outbursts or inspirations. Mine was agreement and evasion: I'd say yes to everything and then flee to the roof to imagine I lived somewhere else, in another body, another year. I'd hear my father's voice from downstairs, feverish, reproachful, grandiloquent, and close my eyes. The darkness clamped between my lids was so intense that it forced them open again. My father never managed to accept his circumstances, and in this sense he deprived us of a healthy relationship with realism.

But that didn't mean he was at fault. In the end, his plans pursued the welfare of his family, not just a boost to his ego. When I think of his omissions and commissions, I hyperbolize the parameters: something full confronted with something empty. And I usually choose the empty end as the site of possibility. My daughterly hypothesis is that my father would have been a much happier man if he'd never had children. In this sense, if you were to be harsh and fundamentalist about it, the blame is ours. My premise is absurd, of course, because it filters my imagined nonexistence through the reality of my existence. I don't know if we were my father's choice or simply what happened to him; many families occurred and still occur out of inertia. I know we were important to him, but we changed from children to audience and from audience to the strictest judges. Humiliation began at home, before we made our way out into the world. We learned to mock my father and then to goad him on with opposing ideologies. Almost every conversation ended in shouting, my father furiously shut away in his bedroom. Sometimes he'd refuse to speak to us, his irascible silence dragging on for days, even weeks. I was always astonished by his ability to enclose himself in a hermetic cage, and by how hard it was for him to leave it once he'd decided to exonerate us. Behind his back, we'd gleefully recount the details of his ventures and place bets on how long the latest tantrum would last.

In these endeavors, my mother, perversely, was our mediator and chief accomplice, and she gradually became the protagonist of our family. Her knack for composure obtained everything that my father's willful whims could not. As the primary victim of his insults and disputes, she drew much of her strength from our compassion. I have no doubt that she exploited this position. Sometime in my teenage years, I trained my hostility on her complaints and began to see her, through a highly schematic kind of feminism, as weak and submissive. My brusque response was that she should leave my father. I even came to imagine their separation as the ideal scenario for everyone. My ungenerous utopia culminated in a family trip we took to visit my maternal grandmother in California. One night, my parents fought with nearly physical violence. Standing behind the grille of the kitchen door, I watched them tussle and wrench at each other in the yard. My grandmother herded us into her bedroom as she prayed to her god that he would keep us safe. The next day, my father appeared and asked my mother, in our presence, if she wanted a divorce. I concentrated hard, willing my mother to say yes. But that's not what happened, and family life remained a matter of balance under threat.

I'm not sure whether my mother was faithful to a man or to a duty. I suspect it was the second. She was the sort of person who unshakably committed to her decisions, who couldn't even conceive of breaking a pact; her moral fiber relied on the bond outliving the obstacles. The determining factor in her relationship with my father was no longer love, but something else: a passion for continuity. The conviction that if it didn't make it to the end, it had never gotten anywhere at all. Maybe she also had a weakness for reconciliation. You can develop a taste for that kind of indulgence, abandoning your pride, assenting to absolution. My mother was an artist of forgiveness: she'd grant it immediately, unconditionally, and wouldn't revisit or rehash a fight. I think her genius was a kind of persistent ethics. She never stooped to shifting with the circumstances, but rigorously obeyed whatever laws she'd laid down at the start: simple and austere, like an ancient canon. Her secret was to never gauge other people's reactions before exercising her own, which was always exactly the same. That's what being a good person must be. And she was one, nearly fanatically so; that's why I felt her actions must follow a strategy of some sort. My father was erratic, original every single day. My mother, by contrast, was homogeneous, predictable. Both were seduced by a single question, a single goal: which of them would be their children's favorite in the end?

Maybe they would have found satisfaction without this rivalry. Their relationship was fractured by four children: six people in a space dreamed up for two. Our predatory presence ousted them to the edges, and they had to get used to watching us from uncomfortable front-row seats; they were forced to act invisible. There, on the edges of things, the distance between them grew. By the time we were teenagers, they were completely opposite each other, jostling for our attention. Fighting reunited them. They sought our testimonies so they could point fingers and exchange the warring accounts that would make them a whole couple again, completing their own circumference without any outside actors. But it never worked that way. The parents became their children's children, and by the time they were invited back into lives, they'd forgotten all about the early episodes. There was no one left who could tell the disjointed story to the family's benefit.

When I picture my mother without children, I imagine a delicately individual, deliberate life, a woman who doesn't see her private plans as a sacrilege. You can't take anything away from someone who has gotten what she wants. In this imaginary concord, happiness brushes against unhappiness in a purely personal plane: there is no responsible or irresponsible progeny. Without children, your roots never set. You float backward and forward, freedom as fleeting as subjection—yes today, no tomorrow. The misfortune of routine depends on no one else. My mother and my father would have stayed together out of a sentimental clarity, not the hazy chaos stirred up by children, as if disarray were the engine of collective overcoming. I can catch a glimpse of my mother on some harried day, piles of clothes to iron, unmade beds, kitchen counters piled with dirty dishes, scolding herself "How did I get into this mess?", reviewing her life until the moment when the first daughter was born and everything seemed to start happening anonymously, no longer to her, but to some woman dressed up as a mother. Four children later, I can sense her regret, despite her absolute and famously unconditional love, her plans making their slow shift toward longing. I can see her steady in a day-dream where she didn't postpone herself indefinitely, as if there would be room, later, to restore what had been truncated or parasitized by motherhood. Where does a person end up in all that?

In his essay "Fires," Raymond Carver confessed that the primary influence on his work was his children, not Hemingway or Joyce or any other writer. He didn't mean a positive influence, in the sense that his children provided him with a constant, joyful sense of inspiration. He meant a negative one: the constant plunder, the time corroded, distorted, cannibalized. This brutal reality came crashing down on him at a Laundromat as he waited his turn to use a dryer. He realized that the rest of his afternoon would dissolve into the frenzy of fatherhood, his consciousness besieged by his children's demands. My parents, in the context of their own aspirations, must have experienced something similar multiple times a week, leaving the grocery store or getting us ready for school: a dislocated, uncentered bewilderment, their own selves already fragmentary. Carver also confessed that he wrote stories instead of novels because he was a father. It must have been gradual, his renunciation. A short sentence instead of a long one; a plot with a visible, perfunctory ending. Someone could interrupt him at any moment to ask for more of this, less of that. My father concocted projects, and his haste to execute them was destructive; my mother read books and magazines late at night to refocus a knowledge diluted by discontinuity. In all three examples, children were the perpetual owners of each falsely personal life, and the barter, where there was one, was always unequal. The possession was far from mutual. I remember it more as a snatching-away: this much Dad and this much Mom for you, this much for me. Only scraps were left, specters shutting the doors and switching off the lights. Twenty-four-hour service. I could hear them from my bed: them, my parents.

But my description or sensation doesn't seek to prove anything. Certainly, not having children puts you in a curious position, without distractions or detours, in full dominion of something that may be impossible to grasp. You belong to yourself, and in the end you may realize that your persona dims if you don't put it at risk; you start melting away into a nervous, perfectionist mind. The influence of childlessness may be even more shocking, a deprivation so intense that it triggers hallucinations of a crowd as you rummage around, hearing no one's noise. A fictitious identity, if forced and constant. While there's no room for regret—you can't undo what was never done—there's an extravagant kind of nostalgia. You miss the future, not the past. As if that conjugation had been erased by a single quandary, that of an adult who wakes up thinking of herself: "What will I give myself now?"

No option is superior to the other. It all depends on what side of anguish you're on. I saw my parents regularly succumb in their daily war with their children. I saw them exhausted, resenting the choices that had been deceptively attributed to free will. At the end of the day, though, we were theirs, even though the equation was unjust and worked to their detriment. We were their people, which must have granted them some kind of tribal, atavistic solace. On the level of instinct, there must be nothing more tempting than family, like founding a country or discovering a new land. Misguided pleasures of biology, first and foremost, and then affection. The rest is fate or fatality—or just luck, if you're superstitious and choose chance as your creed. Family, my family, always made me fearful of overpopulation. There were too many of us under the same roof; real solitude was impossible. The voices stretched into the halls and there was always someone, somewhere, being him- or herself, very much despite and in opposition to the others. Whenever I found myself contemplating the prospect of children, the thought of a full house so stupefied me that I opted for the mystery, or the monotony, of uninhabited space. Age is almost never included in these considerations: youth chooses what old age later laments for its selfishness. Or something like that. It's impossible to calculate when you'll start to feel the consequences of a decision you made decades before. I don't wish I'd had children—I'm certain of that—but I can sense the anomalies of my condition, like a shadeless tree that no one comes to lean against or relax in the company of. There's melancholy in the paltry foliage that kept everything to itself and failed to measure the droughts. As if this metaphor weren't limited enough, I'd add the sky, too: the absence of witnesses to gaze up and make comparisons between clouds and things. All for the sake of sinking into memory or childhood. That's where the visible and invisible children must be.

The past is proportional to its forgetting; you remember what's left. When I think of my parents, it's their deaths, not their lives, that linger on the surface, as if I could only reach the beginning through the end. The challenge is to keep track of them. Every death, moreover, contains the key to its life. Will had everything to do with my father's. He was diagnosed with cancer of the tongue in 1988; true to form, he refused conventional treatment and insisted on an alternate route. He ineffectually injected himself with snake serum for weeks. Once the cancer metastasized, he devoted himself to dozing off and drinking wine. He couldn't speak, so he communicated by writing messages in a notebook I found among my mother's things when we packed up the house. The memos were emphatic. Sometimes, in a kind of truce, he'd remark on the street noise or what we should buy for lunch. Once he was terribly ill, my father coordinated his death with his cardiologist. It was all carried out right on schedule: there were sedatives, then a weeklong coma. My father woke only once, but we showed up late with my mother that day, so only the nurse was there to witness it. We missed his last words. It was normal for us to fail him in this way: in the details. No one betrayed the script.

My mother died eleven years later, adrift, despite her medical obedience. In the terminal proceedings of her illness, an invincible pancreatic cancer, she fell prey to her own modesty. She never managed to overcome her good manners, and she found it impossible to organize the negligible information her doctors provided her. Thinking of her death, talking about it, was tantamount to a breach of trust, and she abstained from referencing any outcomes at all. A few days before she died, she dreamed her mother came to collect her, urging her along: "Come on, Joan, let's go, it's time." It was the only moment I ever saw a premonition break her. She spent her days in the living room, in an armchair, surrounded by her cats, the black one nestled in her lap, her favorite. We took her to the hospital when she could barely walk, on the eve of her death. That night, strangely cheerful, she tried to remember the name of a movie she'd liked. We couldn't help her. She resigned herself to the mystery and then fell silent until the middle of the next day. She died while having her stomach pumped. In her case, we were present for her last words. They were concrete and referential: "This is an instrument of torture." And she politely bowed her head.

I know I'll be a daughter forever—a nearly perverse condition for an orphan. Although it does encourage straight lines, no shortcuts. Me-with-myself isn't a tautology; it's just one of many possible solutions. It's all about determining the nature of the problem.

5.

THE INFATUATED INSTINCT FOR PAIN

0

The body stretches in the bed, the eyes open, they take
in the curtain and the thread of daylight reaching taut all
the way to the white wall, the hands push back the sheet,
the feet seek the ground, the body sits and stands at last,
slips into its slippers, takes a few steps, goes into the
bathroom, pees, observes its face in the mirror, combs its
hair, rinses its mouth, cinches its robe, emerges into the
dimness of the room, regards the shapes of the furniture,
the unmoving plants, and feels the first brush of sorrow,
a slight ache at the height of the solar plexus. It's been
familiar with the sensation for years, although it doesn't
know where it comes from or what triggers it, just that
the body compensates more or less unconsciously, in
that the feeling grants the body a strange certainty of its
essential connection to the world, to the world's very
bones. The pain seems compassionate: toward others,
toward life in its most inclusive, never personal dimen-
sion. The mind, enduring it, never thinks of what concerns it individually or directly, doesn't tell itself, "I

hurt"; it just lets itself be invaded by a series of almost prefabricated emotions that, in the long run, when the experience is over, leave it convinced that it's profound and sensitive and perceptive and not even vain, because that exempts the sadness, whose content varies little and is full of topics: the senselessness of life plunging head-long toward death, futility, the fleeting passage of time, uncertainty, the innocence of immersion in nature, injus-tice, lost causes. It arrives all together, a bouquet of dry flowers that crumble with the slightest touch. It's a sort of species-pain, almost an instinct.

The first time it happened to me, I was around six-teen years old, and I'm sure the initial shock of it con-vinced me I was a special case. I learned to pay attention to my feelings and to the boredom that filtered them out. I learned to contemplate my moods objectively, as if they'd transpired outside me, on a screen that was a rain-streaked window. I learned to use abstract words that resembled thoughts, but which were actually sim-ple vocabulary. I learned to read certain books like man-uals for melancholy. I learned to cultivate silence in my observation of others and empathy as a form of modesty, although, deep down, I believed that others didn't grasp the seriousness of things, "how sad it all is," and a rush of tenderness led me to a conclusion: that of my own goodness, and, of course, my own superiority, because while others spoke and acted, I bore the entire burden of their lives. Which were absurd, and only I could under-stand them. Hence the keenness, the lucidity of pain.

Curiously, joy lacks philosophical weight and we seldom stop to analyze it. It collects, externalizes, com-municates, and rises to the surface, while sadness iso-lates, internalizes, silences, and sinks. We think we know each other better when we suffer than when we celebrate, and sorrow for the world makes us feel more intelligent, more sensitive, especially when the pain is raw matter, sheer perspectiveless emotion. Then we turn on our heel, scorn empathy as saccharine, and make our way toward a kind of sarcasm, of derision; toward the construction of an atmosphere, a scene. That's when sadness gets professionalized. It perfects its language, builds entrances and exits, gestures, signs, and a self-deprecation that fashions its own mechanisms of laughter and remoteness. In sum, it becomes literary, with ample resources at its disposal.

I owned many books that taught me, among other things, how to suffer inside an aesthetic structure with-out ever sacrificing style. Several of these books became my scripts. At various points of my life, I adhered to the laws of their characters, not the rudiments of my own self, which always struck me as a flat parody of what-ever happened on the page. In their documentations of pain, two books and half of a third were essential—not because they were my favorites, but because it was easy for me to grant them a pithy sense of realism and adapt them to my everyday environment. Reading them meant reading myself, later, as I pondered things in my room or scrutinized adults in hopes of entrapping them in one of their many oversights and being able to tell myself, "Of course they don't get it, poor things, they think this is life . . ." And the sketch of an imaginary city evolved in my head, and I saw myself walking away toward its outer limits, which meant the ocean or a river. And I was older; that is, I'd grown tired of wandering the earth and I'd shut myself away, smoking in my little hovel in the evenings, contemplating the open sky, grasping, once again, the insignificance of it all—but with a faint smile, a trace of more or less ineffable wisdom, because if someone had asked me in that moment what I knew, I would have struggled to explain. Maybe it was a kind of annoyance with a deadly conclusion—nothing is worth it—I never truly managed to fulfill: the happy animal inside me urged me on, always coaxing me to give it another chance. And that's when I'd transgress my scripts.

1

The first essential book was *Nausea*, by Jean-Paul Sartre. I read it with preemptive reverence (the author was French, and we all wanted to be French in those days), clutching a pencil so I could underline the cathartic bits, the places where Antoine Roquentin and I envisioned the space of a single experience. It wasn't hard to emulate Roquentin. According to my reading at the time, the book's major theme transpires inside him, while the town of Bouville serves as his theater, his accompaniment. An affliction (protagonist of the book and of that phase of my adolescence) suddenly befalls him: "Something has happened to me, there can no longer be any doubt about it. It came like a sickness, not insistently but slowly and insidiously; I felt a little uneasy, that's all." Roquentin recalls a walk along the beach, the incident of a pebble in the palm of his hand that repulsed him somehow: "And how unpleasant it was! And it came from the pebble, I'm sure it oozed out of the pebble in my hands . . . a sort of nausea in the hands." The physical impression was gradually confirmed: Nausea was a state, a temporal schema, a substitute for the soul.

Roquentin suffers it as a symptom of something worse. His daily activities hardly change. He lives in Bouville because it houses the archive of the figure he's studying, one Monsieur Rollebon. More sublimely, he lives in Bouville because he thought it would be a good place to carry out his life's project: to attain freedom through ataraxia. Bouville was preceded by various trips, time spent in exotic places, a relationship with Anny. Now Roquentin is a monotonous man; he goes to the town library every day, to Mably café, to the bistro Rendez-vous des Cheminots, and he walks. He has a lover, Françoise, to whom he makes love "out of courtesy." He also has an acquaintance, the Autodidact, who is reading the books in the library in alphabetical order (he's in the Ls at the start of the novel) and wants to hear all about what he fervently calls Roquentin's "adventures." Roquentin refuses, however—"Nothing happens when you live"—and offers postcards and photos to appease him.

Sartre's book is Roquentin's diary. It begins on Monday, January 29, 1932, and ends a few weeks later, when Roquentin leaves Bouville for Paris. His pilgrimage includes several stations, several motives, several ways in which his thinking ironically sets its own traps: Sundays, perfect moments, three o'clock in the afternoon, freedom, adventures, experience, fear. I adapted them to my circumstances. Hating Sundays wasn't difficult. They're unbearable everywhere. Mornings last longer, and there's a placidity that unsettles even the light. You can lean over the balcony and see that there's no one on the street, but you can still hear the hubbub of families in the distance, out for a stroll. In my neighborhood, Coyoacán, those noises were archetypal, cut from the same cloth. Around midday—the perfect time for repulsion—I'd hide myself in my room with the shutters half-closed and reflect on the stupidity, the artifice, the spuriousness of contentment. I'd examine the rough patches on the wall, compare this texture to the inside of my soul, and resent the coarseness of my exception: I'd never be able to live in the instant itself. Like my tutor Roquentin, who always failed Anny in his search for perfect moments and destroyed them by letting them slip away undetected. His distraction was so tenacious that it seemed deliberate. The wasted time, the foolish hours stalked him like dazzling revelations: "Three o'clock. Three o'clock is always too late or too early for anything you want to do. An odd moment in the afternoon. Today it is intolerable." The white sun, a piercing whiteness, outlines objects and exacerbates Roquentin's phenomenological nausea. Imitating this servitude to the minute hand was more difficult for my Mexican student schedule, so I modified the rule: my moment of absurdity would run from 4:00 to 6:00 PM. It had nothing to do with the sun and everything to do with a feeling of lethargy that smeared the streets like a thick coat of paint, softening movement until all traces were blotted out. It was an excess of unreality: my persona was a third-party persona; my voice, vicarious; my boredom, a thing of birds and leaves laced together by the wind in a repetitive rhythm that filled me with a sense of nausea almost as elegant as Roquentin's, though always derivative and conscious. A witnessed nausea.

I followed the book's instructions as I went. To

induce the apathy that envelops Roquentin and reveals the limits of his free will, I delved into passivity. Doing nothing meant confining myself to a sound chamber where the void reiterated itself in echoes. Inside, I could repeat in unison with Roquentin, "All I wanted was to be free"—only to find myself abruptly suffused once again with nausea and conclude, "I am no longer free, I can no longer do what I want." That was the first sign of the affliction. Roquentin's freedom was negative in nature: it existed to do nothing. The nausea sapped it of all meaning, because the present started to matter; so did Roquentin's own existence, his intentions. It's not so much a moral issue as a procedural one. Stagnating in sheer present, subjected by inertia to his will, Roquentin ceases to accompany himself and severs ties with his past, even the past of Monsieur Rollebon, which gives order to his time in Bouville. His memories and History, with a capital H, are made up. There is no adventure, and there are no events except for the immediate ones; experience, which Roquentin doesn't believe in anyway, reeks of death. The risk lies in existing, a truth that hits Roquentin over the head one Monday at three o'clock: "The Thing . . . I am the Thing . . . I exist." The realization leads to the fear and claustrophobia of thought: one is because one thinks and vice versa. "Thoughts are the dullest things. Duller than flesh . . . If I could keep myself from thinking!" But this desire is already a thought. There's no way out. Roquentin decides to hurt himself to determine whether bodily harm can interrupt the course of words in his head. He stabs himself in the palm with a penknife—an instrument that typically folds on contact with the skin, making a cut that barely bleeds and quickly dries. Contemplating the process of his blood, Roquentin resolves to never write about Rollebon ever again. And he flees into the street.

My memory of *Nausea* doesn't include the novel itself, its extreme narrativity. I suppose every age captures what can fit inside it, and what I found most striking and absorbable at sixteen was the most abstract: the invasive and uncomfortable feeling of Nausea. Being symbolic, it's the most naive element of the novel, the most juvenile, which is why it invites identification through intense adolescent solicitousness. My vision was unequivocal, not to mention predatory: I consumed only what felt necessary to me. Rereading the book now, though, Roquentin strikes me as practically a man of action, and he's never alone: a perpetual taker of walks and assiduous diner at cafés and bistros who systematically records what he sees and hears. The novel is often about others and sometimes about Roquentin. Nausea certainly becomes the apparatus that sets the plot in motion. But at the end of the day, life proves its own inevitability, even for an author as dogmatic or didactic as Sartre. The book is ultimately a work of naturalism, with a touch of anguish to make it less credible: the gray that unintentionally brings forth the other colors and fades its own.

My memory also omitted the experience of learning about pain, which is so deeply rooted, so possessive, that it grows all by itself. It ceases to be Nausea; it becomes disenchantment or melancholy or boredom with prophetic or spiritual airs. The teachings that were once habits are now instincts, and whatever unleashes them is usually impersonal. A certain kind of shadow at a certain hour of the day; a certain city-murmur with some hammering nearby; a certain kind of someone else's happiness glimpsed from some street corner where the graffiti-painted wall says something like "Eric loves Vanessa and wants to fuck her"; a certain conversation overheard in some office ("I didn't say, look, do it this way, not like that, and she said that Luis . . . and I said that María and said that Juanito said that Luis and I said no, it was actually María, who told me . . ."); a certain face obstructed by an expression that doesn't match the weather or its own haircut or clothing; a certain dog wandering alone through a park; a certain formulation ("So what you're going to do is you're going to take a left on Insurgentes Avenue," "I mean it was literally like the most adorable thing I have ever seen"); a certain show of tenderness; or myself, for trusting linear time and perking up at some optimistic forecast.

I'm not sure whether Roquentin would have accepted this sensorial chaos as a permanent soul-state. To him, existence meant erasing his identity altogether. By contrast, my instinct is always to reinforce it. Pain becomes, narcissistically, the mark of my difference, even if I later scold myself and remind myself that no one is truly unique and the same thing probably happens to most people several times a week; how else can we be sure that we're ourselves? Plus, instincts probably aren't individual to begin with. I cultivated mine like a garden of extravagant plants, slightly beyond the bounds of simpler warmth or communication, maybe because I often plunged into a shy, wallflowery silence. Later on, I gave myself over to absorbing books voraciously and verbatim, sapping them dry, as if I could never settle for living just one life inside myself. But these explanations are so psychological or comprehensive that they spark another little surge of Nausea or apathy or sadness in me. They make it sound as if I'm cooperating with some sort of shared endeavor, and I think I'd rather imagine myself out of focus. In the end, this freedom—the freedom to imagine ourselves—is unrestricted and has no consequences, except for our own well-being. And what is that, anyway? Roquentin would have said that health is versatile and a rebellious spirit suffers for the sake of it, and because he must, even if he still strives to free his passion and rejoin life's simplest routines.

Even Roquentin had a heart. When he finally resolves to leave Bouville for good, he takes a final walk through the city; a romantic in spite of himself, he visits all his usual stomping grounds. He realizes then that Bouville has abandoned him, and he studies the landscape from an outdoor scene in which he is already an exile. He goes to the library, stops by the Mably café, and then visits the Rendez-vous des Cheminots to say goodbye to his lover Françoise, Madeleine the clerk, and the other patrons. He accepts a drink on the house and listens once again to the jazz record that always brightened the bistro's ambiance. The croon of the saxophone transports him: "And I am ashamed. A glorious little suffering has just been born, an exemplary suffering. Four notes on the saxophone." Enveloped by music, Roquentin confesses to himself that he too wanted to be, just be, and when the singer's powerful voice breaks into the melody, he dares to think that his life might be justifiable after all. And so, disregarding his most loyal followers, the fundamentalists of Nausea, he ruins everything with a glimmer of hope. Once he reaches Paris, Antoine Roquentin will do his part, make an effort, write a book: "Perhaps one day, thinking precisely of this hour, of this gloomy hour in which I wait, stooping, for it to be time to get on the train, perhaps I shall feel my heart beat faster and say to myself: 'That was the day, that was the hour, when it all started.' And

I might succeed—in the past, nothing but the past—in accepting myself."

You are you and the other is the other. Is this what we have to accept? Or that life is what it is? I'm not yet levelheaded enough for it. Pain (especially the 6:00 PM kind) helps me mutilate my judgment and disrupt the evidence every night. You can't erase instinct with a single voluntary leap toward reason. You have to do something with all the leftover paraphernalia. And with the costumes and gestures, which remember the body.

2

"I am a sick man . . . I am a spiteful man. I am an unattractive man." With this brutality begins my second essential book, Dostoevsky's *Notes from Underground*. The perception of consciousness, keen as pathology, is unequivocal, and it colonizes the entire dilemma. The narrator is a bureaucrat who, thanks to a modest inheritance, is able to retire as a young man of forty; he lives or subsists in a "wretched, horrid" room on the outskirts of Saint Petersburg. He decides to write his memoirs despite his scorn for any and all conversational partners and his conviction that the book will never be read: "Perhaps it is simply that I am a coward. And perhaps that I purposely imagine an audience before me in order that I may be more dignified while I write . . . Again, what is my object precisely in writing?" Before sharing an early memory triggered by "the wet snow," the narrator addresses his hypothetical readers and establishes the parameters of the drama: he is nothing, because intelligent people can't be anything; that's the job of idiots. It's a neat, clean dividing line. On one side are the (few) people like the narrator, guiltlessly guilty, far too aware, victims of inertia, of suffering. On the other side are the others, the normal ones, people who live in harmony, perform fruitful labors, are positive, seek their own well-being, and tend in principle toward happiness. The narrator mocks them and I obviously took his side. The underground was a room in his head. What could be easier than hiding away in there and speechifying: "And now I'd like to tell you, gentlemen . . . Ha, ha, ha . . ."

This laughter summed up an entire attitude: wounded, acerbic derision. I learned a very different lesson from this book than from *Nausea*: here there was no noble, kindhearted character, more victim than perpetrator, marked by a skeptical humanism, like Roquentin. Here we had a vexed, anonymous, offensive, bitter, resentful narrator, whose distinguishing feature was his raw intelligence—but an intelligence that declares and condemns itself, that works against itself, eats itself alive. What would his lesson be? I'd summarize it in two parts. First, suffering is an inevitable corollary of an incisive consciousness. And second, exacerbated intelligence separates you from others, subjects you to endurance tests that aren't intellectual but ethical; it's the highest form of revenge against any affront. Both lessons come cloaked in a casual, defiant, theatrical tone that allows the narrator to proclaim things like "Every decent man of our age must be a coward and a slave," including himself arrogantly in his insults. Any wound goes to show that he is among the chosen: he sees beyond, he's up above, even if that means being down below, underground, reciting truths like ingredients in a poison. Who cares: the idea is to submit to abysmal, humiliating experiences, so that the propaganda of pain can grow even more urgent. The narrator doesn't relent. His enemies are always hot on his trail. He recounts how, at the age of twenty-four, when he was still working in an office, he did nothing in his free time but read. But sometimes, very late at night, fed up with his own passivity, he'd go out to "[plunge] all at once into dark, underground, loathsome vice." Once, he passed a tavern where two men were fighting with billiard cues. Suddenly overcome with the desire to be hit, he placed himself right in the middle of the brawl. Nobody paid him any mind except for a policeman who wanted to cross the room: he took the narrator by the shoulders and pushed him aside. This so enraged him that he spent days, weeks, preparing his revenge:

running into the policeman on the street and not stepping out of the way. When he finally achieves his goal,
his satisfaction lasts just long enough for him to plan the
next outrageous episode. Like a secular martyr whose
askesis will be intelligence purified by hate.

In the preamble to *Notes from Underground*, the
narrator stretches his theory of suffering to the limit:
"You will be finding enjoyment in toothache next," he
exclaims. At school, in the class where we were assigned
Dostoevsky's book, our favorite object of existentialist
reflections (the class was called Existentialism 101) was,
in fact, toothaches. The argument for the pleasure or
voluptuousness to be found at the heights of acute tooth
pain was, paradoxically, the book's most easily identi-
fiable stance. None of my classmates (nor our teacher)
was prepared to confess the slightest or direst humilia-
tions they'd suffered, but they were more than willing to
tell the class about their dental ordeals. So this became
the most popular collective example of the adverse
path that would work toward the narrator's metamorphosis and our own. For homework, the teacher even
had us write about our worst toothache ever. Some students were literal, descriptive. Others, like me, imitated
Dostoyevsky's narrator and luxuriated in metaphors for
throbbing molars. We knew our spirit was at stake. We
were the buffoons of all that was "sublime and beautiful." Boasting about pain was our greatest victory.

It was just a hop and a skip from there to subversive intelligence. Dostoevsky's narrator hides out underground, lists his grievances, and cures himself with a single mantra: "I am more intelligent, more highly developed, more refined in feeling than all those who wrong me." But no one notices. The subversive part is the spectacle, the show. Witnesses to intelligence are scorched by its radiance; they can't stand it. That's what you think. Once alone, you revel in it again: ha, ha, ha. And again: no one notices. Except for the intruder. When the narrator returns home after a terrible incident with some old friends and a prostitute, he thinks reality will forget what has happened, because there's no one underground to depict it (unless you count his servant, Apollon). Then, relatively calm, he puts on his old padded robe and sits down in his wretched sitting room to read and continue "[imagining] everything from books." But then Liza appears, the prostitute, and exposes the sordid life of the narrator, whose only weapons are hysteria and insults. "Which is better," he wonders, "cheap happiness or exalted sufferings?" The answer is so obvious that not even the narrator dares write it down. There's a final act of revenge: to put a stop to his *Notes*. He'll keep drafting them, he clarifies, but not for readers.

What about the wet snow? That's what survives outside, aboveground, once the passersby, horses, wagons, vendors, and the silence of the resulting water are removed from the equation. Dry snow would have been a perfect stage for heroism: the wet snow is where the extravagant paradoxalist slips and falls and slashes his mask as if it were a manuscript: read my face before I lose it. Literature that ends in shouting has a melancholy effect, like wet snow. So it is, sometimes, with external landscapes: we grant them so much introspection that they turn personal.

3

My third (or, to be more precise, half of my third) fundamental book was Lawrence Durrell's *Justine*, the first volume of *The Alexandria Quartet*. A novel of names, not plots. A novel of characters: Justine ("arrow in darkness"), Nessim ("smooth gloves, face frosted glass"), Purswarden, Scobie ("piracy"), Balthazar ("fables, work, unknowing"), Clea ("still waters of pain"), Mountolive, Pombal, Melissa ("patron of sorrow"). All are extraordinarily intelligent, cultured, and refined; all smoke countless cigarettes and drink for hours without passing out; all are hurt or will be hurt; all are mysterious and have lived motley, complex lives that prompt them to utter sentences marked by both bitterness and wisdom; all flutter like blind pigeons around Justine. And I imitated them.

At sixteen, I found her irresistible: a beautiful, powerful woman, enigmatic and promiscuous and pure and totally honest in her cruelty and deceit. She'd make love with everyone, and afterward, sitting on the edge of the bed with a cigarette between her lips or fingers, she'd whisper precepts about eroticism, the gods, the city of Alexandria, the Greeks, and the urgent need to be alone. A bedroom utopia. That's what the shadowy part of my future looked like to me. Justine was the precursor to La Maga in Cortázar's *Hopscotch*, but without the latter's spontaneity or magic spell of coincidence. She just had the moral acrobatics that let her conceal the repercussions of her actions and dupe her companions. I longed for that freedom as I read. To fall in love with Justine was to transcend middling commitments. It was total submission or nothing, although she continued to barter with her presence. My dream was to become the pursued and not the pursuer, like Justine. How could I achieve her haughty arrogance? Justine doesn't care if she loses what she has, doesn't fret about being betrayed, because her interpretation of the facts will always absolve her of participation in the first place. She moves faster even than her own experience. Or she comes back from it. It doesn't matter, because she never succumbs to the vulgarity of examining her own conscience. She's above all that, and those of us who adore her can only watch as she drifts away. Smoking, flying . . .

–

The doorbell rang insistently. I stopped reading *Justine*. It was the middle of the day, the middle of my summer break. I went to open the door; a man in a navy blue suit asked if my dad was home.

"Can I ask who wants to see him?"

"Mr. Sánchez Ortega."

I went to find my father. He and the suited man spoke in low voices that gradually escalated into complaints and imprecations. The man left him some documents and said he'd be back. My father burst into the living room, distraught. My book was open on the couch.

"What a mess," he said to no one in particular.

My mother materialized from another room. "What's going on?

"The landlords' lawyer . . . that I haven't paid the rent in months . . . he claims I . . . I'm going to call Alfaro . . . he has my payment receipts . . ." My parents rented the property where they ran their restaurant; we were living upstairs by then.

I shut the book and placed it on the coffee table. My dad called his lawyer, Alfaro; the secretary said he was out of town.

"When will he be back?. . . you don't know . . . I need to speak with him . . . it's really urgent . . . please, if he calls you, tell him to get in touch with me . . . thank you . . ."

"What should we do?

"I don't know, I don't know . . . The guy said that if I don't have thirty thousand pesos by 4:00 PM they'll dump everything out on the street."

His lawyer never got back to him. My father contacted some friends for a loan. One friend offered to pay the sum he needed, but in dollars. My dad went to pick up the bills and then to the bank to change them. It was three o'clock. Half an hour later, Mr. Sánchez Ortega rang the doorbell with a notary public.

"How's the money coming along?"

"My dad's on his way home, he's almost here . . . it's only three thirty."

Fifteen minutes later, some ten men vaulted the restaurant patio wall and began to clear out the kitchen, the refrigerators, the freezers, pushing the tables and chairs toward the exit.

"But it's not time yet . . . there's still a few minutes left," my mom protested.

They smiled and didn't answer. At five minutes to four, they hauled the chairs and tables out to the street. The notary started drawing up his document. My father appeared in a taxi with a roll of bills.

"Here's the money, here it is!" he yelled to Sánchez Ortega.

"Well, too late . . . the notary already signed the certificate."

The notary public hurried toward a moving car and threw himself inside. The car screeched off. The ten men unloaded everything else into the street: the food, the rest of the furniture, the kitchen utensils, the dishware, the coffee makers, everything piled onto the sidewalk. By six, the restaurant had been boarded up and we stood guard over our belongings. Neighbors crossed the street; some pointed at us. Close to eight, the moving truck pulled up and took everything to a storage unit. We divided the food among the restaurant staff. The next day, strangely euphoric, my dad placed an ad in the newspaper: "SIXTY-YEAR-OLD ARCHITECT OFFERS HIS SERVICES. DOES EVERTHING. INTERESTED PARTIES CONTACT 24-89-39." He kept it up for days; no one ever called.

When the doorbell rang that day, I was just starting to delve into the shadowy passageways of *Justine*, trying to familiarize myself with the labyrinthine prose of perpetual returns, analogy after analogy, bewildering epigrammatic sentences. Justine had disappeared in the dead of night. The narrator and her husband, Nessim, found her in a brothel of underage girls, caring for a feverish young prostitute. Years later, when I read *The Alexandria Quartet* in its entirety, I learned that Justine's own daughter had been kidnapped as a small girl, and Justine, when she'd had a lot to drink, would rush out in a fit of desperation and search for her in brothels. She'd comfort the girls.

Suffering this way, with many witnesses and devotees to document one's actions, appealed to me. The instinct for pain wasn't brave, just reactive. *A posteriori*, one stage at a time, a literature came into being, forged with quotes that were oracles or promises. Here's one I'll make my own, spoken first by the narrator of *Justine*: "As for me I am neither happy nor unhappy." That must be nice.

6.

CATS AND "I"

1

In the presence of cats, I've always cast myself into question, put myself in quotes: an automatic, intuitive response that suspends and absorbs me, puts me at the mercy of the absurd. Cats, after all, have mastered absurdity like no other creatures. They seem to exist in an alternate regime, a place where logic is always optional, never necessary; where they live without ever grazing against immediacy, in a time midway between the past and the present, in a crack where they basically lurk, play, or sleep.

I guess that's the true meaning of *engatusamiento* in Spanish: a word for the act of tricking or the effect of being tricked or cajoled, and which contains, surreptitiously, a trace of *gato* (cat) in its midst. Ensnaring-by-cat, we might say. I'm sure I'm not the only victim. For some reason, though, I'm unconsoled by the company; cats don't seem to have any shareable, transmissible consequences. In the process of *engatusamiento*, you're alone, your soul is alone with the cats' souls. It's not a trance, nothing quite so magical as that. But it's a place mined by eyes, by gazes: no other animal stares quite so much or quite so well or quite so steadily as cats, and that's where the trouble begins. When they enter a room, when they step across a windowsill, when they sleep on a narrow edge or lick themselves and wash their faces and ears with their tongue-dampened paws, I look at them and they look back and we get stuck there until I half close my eyes and they imitate me and a perfect feline moment arises. Then the cats carry on with their business and "I" linger awkwardly in the introspection of pupils and irises, trying to catch their attention again, but as they're masters of indifference and this rarely happens twice in a row, "I" pet them if I can, tease their whiskers, gently smooth their tails through my closed fingers, and they almost always make their exit. As if I'd crossed a line, broken some unspoken rule; for example, the fact that I live in their space and not the other way around, and there's no touching allowed unless they say so. Something strict that I invariably transgress.

It's not easy to explain my fascination. I've been asked with surprise, condescension, disapproval, repugnance: why do you like cats so much (and dogs and birds and bulls, etc.)? I sense a tacit judgment, an insinuation that all of these sentiments could be channeled into more solid values, into a more classic love for human beings, especially for children. As if, in loving cats (and that's all it is), you were taking something away from people, exhibiting a moral flaw, revealing a perversion. As if, in being attached to an animal or defending its cause, you were excluding someone else from the same pact. "People are what's important, people who are suffering and dying of hunger, not some stupid cat or stupid dog," they say archly. I think there's an equivalence at work: in a system of values that treats a dog or cat as "stupid," human lives must also be worth little, which makes animal cruelty seem trivial or even entertaining—"Let's kick the dog, let's set off fireworks at the cat and see what happens"—and everyone laughs when the animal writhes or yelps with pain. The cases are countless. They break something in me. What's strange is that I feel obliged to justify my compassion as a sort of a breach, a frivolity. What's also strange is that I end up stumbling over my own fervor, and my fondness becomes a form of activism. Or, in certain mocking eyes, of hysteria.

So I'd rather skip the explanation and get tautological: I love cats because I've always loved them. And then I quickly restore them to the center of things, like subjects of emphasis, because there's no better antidote to solemnity than cats. They're the animal outcome of irony, the final flair of laughter. Observing them, I don't see them as Penates, but as guardians of the exquisitely superfluous, of beauty interlaced with muscles and softness and silence and fur. "Cat," I say to the cat, and sometimes he turns around. "Cat," I tell him again, and he stalks off to hunt some nothing. But he doesn't leave my mind. He's proof that the interstices do exist, the regions of meanwhile. That's where we keep each other company, cats and "I."

2

Black cats, calico cats, orange cats, tabby cats, white cats, gray cats, wild, playful, affectionate, standoffish, pugnacious cats, alive today, dead tomorrow, vanishing and reappearing with equal aplomb, here one day, there another, cats who came and went in the garden and backyard of my childhood house like the air's impeccable shadows.

There were two primary periods. In the first, each external section had its corresponding measure of cats: three or four per area, around twenty in total. Some made it so far as to secure a name; anonymous others simply covered up the sun-voids on the floor tiles. But there were never too many for me. I'd go out to play with them, admire them from a distance, attempt to tame the most fearful among them. There were always rewards: cats who approached me, even recognized me the next day. These weren't possessive relationships, though. None of the cats was mine. There was nothing monogamous about it; it was sheer territorial promiscuity. The cats were part of the house, and I suppose the house protected them.

The problem was always my father, who loathed cats with an incomprehensible rage. He saw them as the mere counterpart of mice and rats: sometimes handy to have around, but usually unctuous and disloyal. He didn't understand why you'd want to pet them, how you could feel anything like affection for an animal that lived practically stuck to the ground. The war was constant, and it was waged almost singlehandedly by my mother, who defended cats as if they represented us on the paternal front. My father would put his foot down: no cat could enter the house, and if we dared to sneak one in as contraband, the sanctions would be colossal. Outdoors, there were no restrictions. We reluctantly accepted the deal, but on many afternoons, if my father was out, my sister and I would smuggle our favorites into our bedroom and lavish them with such devotion that the cats themselves found it all a bit much. My father never got any of his children to share his distaste; we all turned out to be cat fanciers, animal lovers. My mother won; the cats won, obviously. Their complicity amounted to both sides of a single coin: "Cats equals mother," my most rudimentary Lacanianism would say.

But a trip ruined everything. My mother took my

three siblings and me to spend part of the summer in the US. For some reason, my father decided not to come along. I remember thinking, as we said goodbye to him, that I might never see him again. The trip felt like a kind of schism: a parental scuffle over their children's heads. I can't remember how long we were gone; probably three weeks at most, although my memory maps an entire season in my grandparents' yard. Back home, everything had changed: we no longer lived in a house, but in a simulation of an apartment, tiny, although the terrace was nothing to sneeze at. Little by little, we gathered the details of the disaster: my father and the gardener had killed all the cats while we were gone.

We wept and cursed my father. My mother excoriated him. I never heard him explain himself, but his silence felt triumphant. Domestic peace was gradually restored—until a cat appeared on the terrace. We fed it and it came back. Within a few months, the feline population had grown, as had our sense of normalcy. The battle of wills with my father resumed; the restrictions returned, the decisive distinction between indoors and out. It was the beginning of a new age and its proper quota of cats, which were now more mine, more conscious than before.

This second period had a different rhythm: slow, verbal, precise. It also coincided with my teenage years and the burden of rebellion to which I subjected myself

like a sickness. But there were always cats. I'd read on
the terrace, surrounded. They'd look at me and I'd look
back and that was enough for a kind of shared passion to
emerge. Most of them had a name. More than one name:
the spoken-out-loud name and the whispered names
that usually ended in onomatopoeias. Pronouncing
their variants was as pleasurable as singing a song: my
voice comfortably settled into a perfect niche, the cat-
niche and its special spell, its incantation of presence,
of wandering around and stretching suddenly like a bow
unfolded on the terrace floor, in the sun's most exacting
spot. I'd lift my eyes from the book and feel immersed in
the circumstances of the cat, not my own, and that was a
solace. Like reaching the farthest shores of a warm place
and resting there. I'd murmur my favorite name, "cat,"
and close my eyes with the book in my lap and the word
suspended between the page and the fluff of the air. The
cat was the passing of time around the edges. The kind
of time that no one counts but that operates beneath
the surface of the minutes. It slips away at the slightest oversight, and the cat startles and chases something
along the top of the wall, on a ledge, under a tree; not
birds, but flutterings of dust and dry leaves and lizards
motionless on rocks. Sometimes a cat would catch one
and play with it, letting it go, catching it again, studying it, tossing it into the air. In the name of the common good, I'd convey it to safety. Afternoons with cats

sometimes involved corpses. Any motion was a challenge and a risk. If the cat won, there were spoils. The hunt was so lazy that it seemed like a dream and you had to wake up in time to keep from becoming an inadvertent accessory to death. Then the cat or cats would go back to sleep and I'd read with the shifty perception of eyes in wait.

Months later, there was another cataclysm. We lost our house again, and my father, exasperated, brandishing some pointy object in the air, imposed a condition: we would only be allowed to bring two cats to our next home. The others (there were something like fifteen by then) would stay behind. There were afternoons of violent weeping. We'd go out to the terrace to survey the population, rearrange the list of the chosen few. Finally, we let chance do the choosing, letting the randomness of proximity make the call: we'd take whichever two cats happened to be on the terrace on moving day. The rest would have to cope with the disaster as cats do: in hiding. We never accumulated them again. Family losses joined feline ones: one of the chosen cats died and the other went astray, waylaid on some foreign wall when we moved to a more definitive house, following the maternal baton. I felt all those cats in the wake of emptiness that followed. When the dog appeared, I couldn't shake my habit of stroking silhouettes instead of bodies, and I came to accept the dog as you might accept a clumsiness: with both affection and resentment. My eyes kept scouring holes and hollows. Where was there a cat who could fill them? The dog wagged his tail in the air, where a cat's shadow was supposed to be, and that faint breeze was a comfort in my quest for tiny, insignificant lives. The dog did become my dog in the end. I held him very close to my heart, very deep within— until, one day, someone opened the front door without noticing the tail and he shot out into the street and a car flung him to the sidewalk in a pool of blood.

To mourn an animal is to practice compassion without pretexts, without histories. The pain makes no demands. It's nearly pure, and so there's nothing you can barter with to make it better. My friends looked at me, puzzled, eyebrows raised, thinking, surely, "Poor thing, why is she so worked up? It's just a dog." But the "just" explained the empathy: an animal never knows. An animal trusts absolutely in her owner, in the person she's supposed to follow or obey. To harm or neglect her is tantamount to abusing that trust, betraying the powerful connection forged between your gaze and hers. The expression is genuine: every animal has a face. How can anyone hurt something with a face? Words are useless, because they quickly morph into a kind of ideology, a campaign. Suffice it to say that perceiving another creature's anguish is more than enough reason to always act against that anguish.

The dog was replaced by a cat, a Siamese cat, the only solitary (or purebred) feline I'd had in my now ample menagerie. My weary father relented, although he warned us that there couldn't be any others; there was no time. I ended up leaving home and the country and the cat was forced to find an alternative, another body to spend his nights beside. The bed is the fortress. Cats always choose one. I was privileged that he chose mine. Every night, I felt the cat's soft leap, then the weight of his back against my legs. It became an addiction: without his company, I struggled to fall asleep. That's when I realized how easy dependence is when nerves make the rules. And that I was barely master of myself. When I said goodbye to the cat, touched his face, the ridge above his eyes, his cool ears, I asked him to forgive me for disrupting our nocturnal harmony and fretfully tried to imagine what my nights would be like from then on. All those catless beds.

Years passed before the next cat, the first that would be truly mine. And the first I ever bought, from one of the pet stores on the Paris piers. She was black and yellow and fluffy. She got sick and spent her first two weeks in my house on the verge of death. Her convalescence sealed an indelible pact: she belonged to me and I to her. I shrank back to my earlier size, put myself in scare quotes again. The cat slept at my feet for fourteen years, and as the days passed, she intertwined herself with the hours as if she were made of time itself. In her fifteenth year, when she was gravely ill with cancer, we had her put to sleep. I remember the moment when the needle pierced the skin of her front paw, and how she turned to look at me: her final face. Once I dreamed of her while traveling: I was chasing her through a forest and she stopped in a brilliant clearing and looked at me, almost smiling, before she carried on her way. I let her go. And the daytime ache was soothed.

A few weeks later, I visited the US-born poet Gustaf Sobin, a professional cat lover. He uttered an aphorism: "Every life has seven cats." It was his way of convincing me to find a replacement. Strictly speaking, my life had had one cat; I had six to go. I suspected I wouldn't be able to fulfill the quota, since most cats live around fifteen or eighteen years. Now I'm on the second. This one's black and fluffy, too. She has a cold nose and a repertoire of meows worth recording. She's lived an epic life, full of walls and roofs and birds and dogs. Once she got stuck on a neighbor's roof and we set out with real desperation to rescue her.

I'm still not sure who is at whose service. I wouldn't mind confessing my subjugation if it weren't for my aversion to cliché. My "I" dims in the presence of these small, deft quadrupeds who ring the walls like transient ribbons. And my "I" always fears losing them. Which is why its exacerbated consciousness counts them among its obsessions. It's elemental: if it doesn't think of them, it worries they'll stop existing, and then what would "I" do with the emptiness in its head when it's time to find the right cat and have an excuse for postponing everything else?

3

Other cat fanciers have reproached me for my monogamous ways. A true cat-lover, they insist, should have at least two and then gradually appropriate more, out of inertia and by accident, until the environment has become so thoroughly feline that anything human seems like a fluke. But my attachments are so possessive that they can't handle rivalry. Besides, cats aren't gregarious; they don't easily tolerate each other. They dispute territory, provoke and spit. In combat, they lose their ridiculous and irresistible charm. Animalized in this way, they stop playacting to seduce us and devote themselves to defending, by yowl and by growl, the regions won during the night. The spectacle of progress and occupation grows mean-spirited after a few hours. By contrast, the solitary cat has the daintiness of a minuscule announcement whenever she appears in a room or jumps up on your lap or curls up in a nook and then decides, when the sleepless hour strikes, that it's time to play and careen around the house like a realist cartoon. All so you'll chase her and laugh and say "You crazy cat, what are you doing?" and then she'll lick your hand and close her eyes, satisfied by the success of her joke.

Numbers make for mystery and gravity. At the end of her life, my mother, by then widowed, had nine cats. Or the nine cats had her. Visiting her for lunch on Sundays, I always suspected I was interrupting a regime of collective self-absorption. My mother spoke to her cats as if they were her closest confidantes. Cats came and went around the house and she welcomed them back with the special pomp their wanderings accounted for. When she got sick and had surgery and received the bad news of her diagnosis, her first question was "What about my cats?" I know she spent hours in the living room with a large black cat lodged on her lap; I also know that it was this same cat who brought her attention to the rising lump between her ribs. Even in the grimmest moments of her illness, there were always feline absurdities. A constant: when my mother would come downstairs with her wig neatly perched on her head, one of the cats, taking it for some pretentious bug, would snag it, dislodge it, and sometimes yank it off altogether. This was how my mother reconciled herself with her condition, the grief of it. No one else could bring her such delight without a tinge of morality, without words that ruined the transaction. Nine cats can outdo a single person's piety, even if that person is her son or daughter. My mother didn't want our complex messages of solidarity; she wanted simple, immediate acts. Cats here and there. That was enough to distract her.

Populating your life with cats is one possible fate. I haven't chosen it yet. I know I'd wind up deep in a silence like my mother's, my eyes fixed on the floor and its ghosts. I also know that I'd care so much about the cats that people would only accentuate my solitude, which pushes conversation into the imaginary realm. Cats coexist with images like birds with air. When they get into your head, they build passageways and corners, and time goes as supple as their bodies: it leaps, hides, vanishes, and, for a few moments, stops passing altogether. It's the cat that occurs when "I" postpone myself. The cat alone. If I had more, I'd have to multiply my "I," and it would turn into one of my creatures, and I'd no longer know who perceives who and where.

7.

ON HOW GUILT BEGINS AT 6:00 PM
(AND INNOCENCE NEVER DOES)

For many years now, I've smoked my first cigarette between six and six thirty in the evening. And for many years, too, as soon as I inhale the smoke and let it out again, I'm invaded by a sense of guilt both deep and vague. Guilt or regret. As if I'd committed various wrongs, as if the smoke unveiled me, confronted me with a betrayed essence; as if the very act of living meant accumulating indiscretions. When I try to study the sensation, to compromise with it by analyzing my offenses, I find nothing but the certainty that my behavior puts me in debt, that omission is the only possible form of innocence. If I hadn't acted, if I hadn't spoken, if I hadn't decided, I would be innocent.

Throughout the day, I experience more inside my head than outside it, which means that my sins are often mental or emotional ones. That's why I feel guilty for the things I repress, things that I alone am witness to. And I do mean sins. I feel and think reprehensibly on a daily basis, always in relation to others, always in relation to life. For example, I might feel the urge to hurt someone I truly care about, I might think that I deserve more than someone else does—all in the swift current of conscience, without ever acting in accordance with those impulses. No, I control myself, I play the part of my persona-for-everyone-else, the character who always tries to behave in a moral, rational way. But at dusk, with the first mouthful of smoke, guilt passes over me like a cold, slender shadow. As if my nature, radicalized by cigarettes, were pining for an Eden of goodness. Then I investigate, rummage about: where did I go wrong? I review the day from start to finish. Most flaws, I confirm yet again, are committed in speech, because the speaking voice corresponds to someone else, a half-stranger, a wild creature that acts at the edges of me and runs around all by itself, belonging to language, to the species, to the community, a forgotten entity who doesn't know everything it thinks and only finds out when it starts talking. Is it my persona or is it me? There's a margin of chaos between the voice and silence; crossing it breeds the elemental guilt of having crossed it to begin with. If you'd kept quiet, you wouldn't have caused the uncomfortable accident of interpretation. When someone else listens to you, she constructs you, decides you're this or that, manufactures a personality for you—a thorny affair that dissolves when you're alone. And there, inside you, is an undefined, perfectible place, where you'd like to erase all outside impressions, because whoever lives in there isn't described by that gaze, but by this one, the most intimate one, the one that nobody else can see.

But silence doesn't save you. Inside a space that's also full of voices, ambiguous feelings and convoluted thoughts are developed like black-and-white photographs. They're part of the landscape, the weather. As if the passive, introspective personality were made of negative impulses and could only be rectified in its relationship to the world. At the end of the day, morality can't be a solitary resource. It always astonishes me to glimpse what's inside, the quantity not cursed but certainly unconfessable: rage, jealousy, pain, exasperation. Until someone shows up and interrupts the life of your conscience and you put on a show of civility. Which in itself is enough to alter the inner atmosphere, because the other person usually offers a truce, an indulgence, unsolicited yet automatic. And you retreat inside in hopes that another perspective has opened up, a window, the threat or promise of translucence. Who truly sees us? There's the persona (the part we play like a character) and then there's personhood (the person we are); behind them both is the conscience, the soul, the ensemble that might amount to Me. The persona goes out, chats, works, meets friends for lunch. Its spontaneity is as prescribed and as closely monitored as its gestures. It looks at itself as someone else, also in character, looks back. It discovers attributes and reactions. Meanwhile, inner life putters along, and self-censorship ensures that the person-herself doesn't overstep the bounds, doesn't barge in to blurt some truth that might put personae in a tight spot. Back inside, the person-herself starts reviewing things, corroborates that her persona falls short, is a pale imitation of a single-handedly constructed ideal that collapses with the slightest touch. The person always imagines herself as something better. At six or at six thirty, I light a cigarette. When I exhale, guilt overtakes the entire situation. And the trivial scene immediately turns abstract, as if it were a condition evolving into a form of purity, and as if, now pure, it resented the principle of baseless remorse. Remorse for the simple fact of being.

Maybe it's a question of personality. According to Heidegger, the conscience is "primarily remorse" and its voice "speaks" from the certainty of debt. My paraphrase is a transgression, of course. One shouldn't put Heidegger in one's own words. I only subscribe to what I understand. If the conscience is remorse, then a sin has already been committed, which means the conscience exists in retrospect: remembering or regretting reveals its intrinsic nature. In a way, this proves the Biblical thesis of original sin. We're indebted to an origin myth. Guilt corroborates the existence of the god who expelled us, the god we recall with a twinge of capital punishment when we hit bottom (take my cigarette, for example). Although this may sound far too simple, like an act of faith instead of knowledge. Besides, the divine hypothesis doesn't seem to exist in Heidegger. In his work, the being has other things to worry about: anguish, time. First, he must face an initial version of realism, of existing in the world. Later, he confronts a grammar that lets him manifest himself phase by phase, prefix by prefix, in a high-action novel where philosophy is the detective and the corpse is a verbal one: a body we read in search of meaning. We know it exists because that's where the fingerprints are, tribute to an earlier investigation. Heidegger examines the conscience as if it didn't belong to anyone. There must be a garden on the other side, an impeccable stream, a forest beyond. It wasn't for nothing that Heidegger placed poetry at the center of clarity. Ever since, poetry has been forced to struggle with sublime hindrances, grandiloquent deities.

Which doesn't settle the issue of guilt. Maybe it's our nature, our most primitive trait. On second thought, the "we" sounds arrogant; I doubt my dilemma is universal. Montaigne wrote that he seldom experienced remorse and was generally satisfied with himself. This has an *a posteriori* air, however. Not feeling guilty follows from "accepting yourself as you are," which I've never been able to do. My self serves me as a walking stick, not a solace. If I abstain from acceptance, it's because, when I find myself suspended in guilt or self-derision, I open the door onto a utopia. Perfection can be verbal: "I teach nothing," Montaigne asserted; "I simply tell." If you define yourself this way, guilt or regret is a mere accident, protocol, good manners. You grant yourself guilt so you can cede innocence to the other, but it's all on the surface. Inside, meanwhile, you recognize serenely that there's nothing to regret because you are the way you are. That's enough for the scales not to shift, enough for them to stay neutral, balanced. "It is an exquisite life that keeps itself in order in private." This, as he himself describes it, must have been the nature of Montaigne's introspection: organized, transparent, marked by direct, pristine exchanges with the outside world. No character to play, just pure personhood, inside and out. A fully Socratic zone where the catchphrase "know yourself" would have the might of an everyday army: "This is who I am and I am enough." Such a slogan makes no room for guilt. At most, when confronted with a flaw, you'd simply tell yourself "To err is human," pat yourself on the back, and carry on, satisfied.

The anonymity of mistakes is as persistent as the authorship of virtues. From the perspective of my would-be guilt, I've observed that when someone makes a mistake, he generally attributes the fault to the collective, to the norm—but when he does something right, it's a personal triumph, with a full name. Perhaps that's what knowing yourself is all about. Although no one is infinite. How long does self-knowledge actually take? I usually erase it in the name of doubt, as if the razor-blade were a kind of spiritual calisthenics: my I jumping around to keep from cutting itself. "That's how thick the skin is," my "I" concludes; "that's the end of uncertainty." In the space between doubt and the emerging hint of guilt, a promise survives: that the outcome will surpass the premises. Then you can deal with yourself as a perpetual hypothesis—no proof needed. Self-knowledge is indefinitely postponed; first you need to convict and never forgive yourself. An open system, a procedure like a metamorphosis. No fixed substances, only absences. "I'm guilty and this will never be full." Reasons for guilt are the least of our worries. I always have more than I need. I smoke and think: "What did I do wrong today?" The pressure in my ribcage is remorse, and I can glimpse the coordinates when I finish my cigarette. This is the size of the ascent toward innocence. Fortunately, I never reach it.

There's a parody of every episode. To an extent, my guilt is circumstantial; it would probably vanish if I stopped smoking, which would make my reflections entirely useless. Or maybe the guilt is disguised as something else; maybe it's actually my body balking at the nicotine.

The conflict would solve itself if I abstained from lighting that first cigarette. Although, with this immediate benefit, my life would look more like a self-help course, and its goal would suddenly be happiness. No smoke, no guilt. No precipice. There would be vague, lingering memories of everyday rifts, but they would vanish in the lukewarm light of self-complacency. I'd be there, right there, my smiling persona roaming the world, my personhood hidden in my bones. My conscience wouldn't be fractured, and not a single being there would struggle to scale the walls of the day and the night. I'd be me, or something like that. All because I didn't smoke.

I like to invest in essences before cracking jokes. My conviction suggests a primordial guilt: that's the headquarters of identity, or at least of my own. If I were innocent, I'd hear a single voice in my head, the simple voice of a reflection. But the inner crowd takes on all kinds of consequences. In the flux, they all become credible, like river stones that don't change the course of the current. I think my persona is a metaphor for my personhood. I think I'm guilty of inventing it. I think we shouldn't invent analogies for our passions. I think "I" assumes something it doesn't possess. And that's exactly what is never forgiven behind the veil of smoke.

8.

JEALOUSY IN A *VERY* MODERN MIND

If there were a hypothetical list of what makes a modern person, my friend M. would check every box. She's certain that she has no prejudices of any kind, that she's impossible to scandalize. She thinks carefully and always tries to make sure that her decisions don't affect third parties (those famous third parties). She considers herself to be rational, just, even-keeled, tolerant, and open-minded. No one would ever call her conservative or moralistic. On the contrary: people often ask her for advice in difficult situations, and she's unflaggingly principled. But my friend has one problem: she's very jealous. She imagines voices and glances where there are only accidents. And she doesn't know where in her mind or soul they come from. How to make sense of this contradiction? If you're genuinely liberal, which my friend M. thinks herself to be, you can't be possessive. And jealousy is possessive — so forceful when it strikes that it destroys all convictions and good intentions. A jealous person will do anything to discover the truth. And what a word: truth. To the jealous

person, it's hidden in a lie. The jealous person is a herme-
neutist: she deciphers, rummages, untangles. The world
beyond her eyes is infinitely guilty and interpretable. It's
inhabited with a paranoid, investigatory air. To love is to
unearth a crime.

Or something like that, says M., who sometimes
speechifies and sometimes philosophizes, depending
on her mood or source of inspiration. I stop her when
she starts threading generalities. My own temperament
rejects abstractions that lose the subject of a sentence
on the way to some dubious transparency. The dilemma
becomes grammatical, literary. Which means that even
light, surface-level adjustments can correct or dispense
with it. "Examples," I tell my friend. "Give me examples." And she gives me one. It's recent. I should mention that my friend M. has been happily married for
years. The stability of her relationship often sparks envy
in others. Even so, jealousy besieges her.

A dinner party: M. and P. (her husband),
another couple (the husband is Japanese), and
the hostess. The wife in the other couple is
enthusiastic about the wine and the attentions
of P., who is the one serving it that evening.

An abstemious M. sips her glass of water.
The husband in the other couple speaks

a knotty Spanish; the others ignore him ruth-
lessly. He tries to explain that the haiku just
isn't translatable to other languages and cul-
tures. Everyone else agrees and changes the
subject.

P. seems dazzled by the laughter of the wife
in the other couple: the group's primary energy
concentrates there.

M. goes outside to smoke with the hostess
and the husband in the other couple. The hostess asks the man (who is the last to step out) not
to shut the door because she hasn't brought the
key. Strangely, he shuts it.

P. and the wife in the other couple are left
alone inside. Outside, M. smokes nervously and
fast; she hears their laughter. She finishes her
cigarette and starts to rap on the door. They
don't open it. She knocks and then all three of
them knock. No one opens up.

M. gets anxious. She imagines P. inside,
kissing the wife in the other couple, fondling
her, whispering: "Don't open it, wait."

They keep knocking and start shouting:
"Come on, guys, open up already." At last, the
wife in the other couple opens the door, laughing, because P. has said, "What, are you really
so scared you'll lose your husband?"

M. rejoins the dinner with a frazzled heart. She acts as if nothing is wrong, but she obsessively watches P., who pours wine and laughs and makes jokes. The wife in the other couple all but applauds him. The Japanese husband no longer says much, just ventures the occasional grumble or exclamation, looking down at his hands or the tablecloth. M. wants to go home. She signals to P., who glances at her with annoyance, but assents.

As they're saying their goodbyes, M. sees that P. and the wife in the other couple hug. Her heart cracks.

Back at home, M. berates P. They fight. P. denies everything and accuses M. of being jealous and crazy. M. cries. P. slams doors and drawers. They go to bed. Their bodies don't shift toward the center of the mattress.

"What do you think?" M. asks me. "Am I crazy, or did something happen that justified my jealousy?"

It's an odd case, I can't deny it. A closed door: two inside, three out. Anything can happen in an instant: a kiss, a caress, or nothing. P. refuted every accusation, but what else do the rules of cohabitation prescribe? Deny everything, never tell the truth.

I answer M.: "Since there's no way for you to know

exactly what happened, why don't you choose the version that hurts you least? That is, nothing happened. End of story." But a jealous person never does that. It's not in her nature. My well-read friend M. quotes *Othello*: "I never gave him cause," Desdemona insists, and Emilia, Iago's wife, responds: "But jealous souls will not be answered so. / They are not ever jealous for the cause, / But jealous for they're jealous. / It is a monster / Begot upon itself, born on itself." M. goes quiet. Then she recounts the story of Othello so she can explain: all you need to do is plant the tiniest seed of doubt for the jealous mind to gun its engines. That's what Iago does. First he insinuates to Othello that there's something going on between Cassio and Desdemona: glances, attention, flirtation. Othello takes the bait and starts to scrutinize Desdemona, to read her between the lines. Iago stokes the fire: he steals Desdemona's handkerchief, a gift from Othello, and gets it into Cassio's hands. Othello takes this as absolute proof of infidelity. He kills Desdemona. When he learns of Iago's deceit, he can't bear to go on. He commits suicide.

The jealous person is always the victim, M. adds. No one has any patience or sympathy for her. The jealous person is insane, thinks almost everyone who isn't jealous: "It is the green-eyed monster which doth mock / The meat it feeds on," Iago says. But M. requests a place in the realm of reason; can't we at least acknowledge the possibility that she might be right? At the end of the day, she says, infidelity exists, sudden attraction does occur, the chance for a romance on the side does lurk around a couple's life together. Sometimes someone pays a great deal of attention to someone else, who is also accompanied by someone else, and the tense triangle of jealousy snaps into place. The offended person has two options: pretend that nothing is happening and wait for the spark to be snuffed, as Robert Burton suggests in *The Anatomy of Melancholy*, or let jealousy take over and protest, as M. does. Oddly, if you protest, you come off as the guilty one: guilty of a lack of style, of betraying the credibility of a fabrication. The behavior manual—which no one has written and everyone has read—insists that the proper thing, the smart thing, the ideal way to win the match, is to carry on as always. To not even react. To smile at your partner and at whoever's metaphysically winking in their direction.

But M. has never learned how to conceal a wound, to disguise an ache. Why is it socially acceptable to say my head hurts, my stomach, my leg, ouch, you're stepping on my toe, but not to acknowledge the pain of injured virtues? to put it formulaically. M. wears her heart on her sleeve; she can't hide it, wouldn't know where. It's a serious design flaw. Inside and outside are not different places, but temperatures, atmospheres, barely separated by skin.

"All right," M. asks me, "is it more aggressive to cause jealousy or to express it?"

I dither for a while, then say, as if I knew something she didn't: "I guess the best approach would be to do whatever will yield the most positive results. Don't you think? Expressing jealousy usually leads to an argument. Your example proves it. And what's the point of fighting, anyway?"

"Well, it means you get to make up," M. whispers.

Some reward, I think. Hell isn't underground; it burns at brain level. The devil's in the forehead. It must bring the other person some pleasure to receive the curious gift of jealousy. No one's jealous of me: does that make me unloved? Or trusted? Better try another example.

"Do you have one?" I ask M.

She always has one. The jealous person is awash with circumstances; that's what she shuffles around in her head after hours.

M. is invited to a conference or round table or presentation in a small city. She accepts with some reluctance. She'll have to spend a night away from home before she returns the next evening. P. seems pensive when she tells him the news. Then he says, "Well, I guess I'll go see that movie." M. feels a surge of anxiety.

"What time? At night?" "Yeah . . . around six or seven . . ." "Then what . . .? You'll come back home?" "Well, yeah . . ."

M. catches her flight, checks in at her hotel, and calls P. "Are you still going to the movies?" "Yes . . ." "Well, fine . . ." "Why, does that bother you?" "No, it doesn't bother me, I just don't get why you have to go . . ." They quickly soften their tones, murmur terms of endearment, and hang up.

M. takes part in the conference or round table or presentation. She's done around 8:00 PM. The organizers inform her that they won't be able to join her for dinner. M. returns to her hotel, goes to her room, sits on the edge of the mattress, and calculates the hours left until she'll be able to sleep. She goes outside for a cigarette. She returns to the room. She looks at herself in the mirror. She touches up her makeup and decides she'll take a walk around the main square, stop at a café, come back to the hotel for dinner, and then go up to bed.

She's done with dinner around ten thirty. She returns to her room. She thinks that P. must be home by now. She calls the landline. No one answers. She calls his cell. No answer. M. takes off her makeup, washes her face, gets into her pajamas, and calls both numbers again. Nothing. She gets into bed, picks up her book, and tries to read. *Angels*, by Denis Johnson. The novel is so sordid that it's laughable, like a joke told backward. She reads listlessly. Fifteen minutes pass. It's eleven ten. She calls again. No one answers. She leaves a message on the house phone: "Where are you? It's like the third time I've called. And you're not answering your cell. What's going on?"

She tries to read a few more pages. She can't concentrate. She gets up and goes to the bathroom. She decides to keep the light off. In the darkness, she imagines P. with someone, out to dinner or at a bar. Happy, drinking a bottle of wine. She's dressed up for the occasion. P., excitable, makes a toast. He touches Her hand. They drive to a hotel, embrace in the parking lot, kiss in the car.

M. turns on the light. She calls again. No one answers. M. goes out to smoke and calms down a bit. She scolds herself: "Don't be ridiculous, why would P. do that, and with whom . . ."

She gets back into bed, switches off the light. She shuts her eyes: she sees a drunk P. on top of Her voluptuous body. She turns on the light. It's eleven forty. She calls again. No one answers. She leaves another message. "I don't know what to think. I'm really starting to worry. Where are you? Please call me back." Her voice is pitiful. It sharpens. She has tears in her eyes. She turns off the light and pulls the sheet over her head. She tries to relax. She presses her eyes shut and groans. P. isn't like that, she tells herself. The rush of fear: What if he got kidnapped leaving the movie theater? She imagines P. tied up in a trunk, his mouth taped shut, the kidnappers calling the house, her far away. Strangely, the kidnapping causes her less anguish than the infidelity. M. would set out to save P., cool and collected. But if P. is with another woman, M. would have to decide whether or not to forgive him and heal and erase the images from her mind if she were to stay with P. And she doesn't know how to erase.

She grabs the phone and calls again. At last, P. picks up, sounding very cheerful: "Hey! What's going on, why did you leave those weird messages?" "Where have you been?" M. is furious. "I stopped for dinner after the movie. I had some wine." "All by yourself?" "Of course . . ." A brief silence. Both laugh. They send each other sweet, diminutive kisses. M. forgives P. out of sheer relief. They hang up.

M. settles into bed and slowly drifts off. The next day, at breakfast, she tells one of the conference organizers that she'd had her dark night of the soul. He looks perplexed.

"What do you think?"

I don't know what to say to M. The two examples share a blind spot: the closed door, the unanswered calls. I try to put myself in M.'s shoes, although I'm not a jealous person and I struggle to imagine being one. I would have found the closed door entertaining. But the unanswered calls would have made me nervous, less for fear of infidelity than of a mugging or kidnapping. Still, I'm sure I would have been able to fall asleep, and I never would have left messages betraying my unease.

"Why not?" M. asks. "Why wouldn't you express your feelings to the person you're closest to? I don't see the point of playing hide-and-seek . . ."

Should I confess my opinion to M.? Some ancient malformation has me convinced that you should never portray yourself as weak, more invested, more in love. An old voice—an old-school voice—repeats to me: "If someone sees you're trying harder or feeling more, they'll just leave you or humiliate you." I make my confession. M.'s instantly agitated.

"Are you serious? You live with someone and you hide what you feel. Which means you're always strangers to each other. You never really know the other person . . ."

"Something like that," I say.

And we fall silent. I think of the anomaly: M. retracts her trust; I never grant it. My lack of jealousy is a strategy, in fact. I know how to mask it. Or is it that I respect the other person's unassailable independence? That I'm a hippie, that I follow the *I Ching*, that I recite to myself: "Let your horse wander off; if he truly belongs to you, he will return on his own"? Am I any wiser than M., always flailing about in her own emotions?

I try to meet M.'s eyes. She looks back and smiles. She asks if I want to hear her very worst example, the one about retrospective jealousy, the most shameful kind of all. I like seeing her this way. Her sincerity is seductive; it gives her an air of mischief. I ask her to tell me.

M. had just moved in with P., whose house was already very much lived-in. She felt like a guest at first, someone passing through, soon to be on her way. She'd wander through the living room and other rooms like a skittish cat. Sometimes she'd rearrange objects, dust surfaces, plump cushions. Then she'd sit in an armchair and wait for the day to wear on. She only felt at home in the house when P. was with her.

In the bedroom was a tall dresser with many drawers. One day, almost absently, M. started to open them all. One drawer contained stacks of letters. She went through them, trying to see who they were from. Some were from J., P.'s best friend. Others were institutional, from the university, from the embassy. Others were from neutral, unfamiliar people. And then, in a separate pile, were lots of letters from three different women: A., F., and L. M. slammed the drawer shut, certain that something had hurt her. She couldn't find a comfortable way to sit in the armchair, and she was tense with P. that night.

"What's wrong?"

"Nothing . . . I'm just tired . . ."

She slept poorly. She spent all night constructing faces and bodies. A. was surely a brunette, petite, short-waisted, with an upturned nose and enormous breasts. F. must have had thick, curly hair, a mane so richly brown it was almost black, a round, intensely feminine face, blue eyes, a deliciously plump, sensual body. She couldn't get any farther with L. than the hazy image of a rival, although she'd have to be extremely beautiful. Near dawn, M. wept with rage. How could P. have done this to her?

Then she remembered that she and P. hadn't even met yet. She was unconsoled. The wound had nothing to do with chronological reality; it was about the presence of these letters. Only by reading the letters could she be cured. She got to work around noon. The house was still, the sunlight had drifted into the living room, and the bedroom was swathed in cool shadow. M. shut the door behind her, opened the drawer, and took out the letters. She started with the ones from F., the thickest pile:

My love,
I miss you so much. I've been traveling for days and all I can think about is coming home . . .

F. shared details of her stay in Paris. Naturally, she had "loved" the Eiffel Tower. Her punctuation was slipshod. This pleased M., who started skipping paragraphs and reading only the intimate parts: "I want to feel you inside me again," "My body misses you, it needs your mouth, your touch."

M. couldn't believe it. F., though corny, was astonishingly sexual, which pierced her soul like a needle.

With A., everything was different. Her letters were brief, clever, provocative. Sometimes she'd allude to some sexual episode, but she really did seem to be making up her letters as she went. M. hated her strong prose, her intelligence. Her eyes welled with tears. She imagined A.'s laughter, P.'s delight.

As she gathered F. and A.'s letters to start in on L.'s, an envelope fell to the floor. Inside were photos of a naked woman posing in bed. She was pretty, with a svelte body, large breasts and blah blah blah, M. said to herself, overcome with hatred. There was nothing written on the backs of the photos, and the envelope was also blank. M. decided it had to be F. She looked the type. P. must have taken the photos in some provincial hotel, a hotel with creaky beds and dark showers, a hotel in a place like Pachuca or San Luis Potosí. M. imagined the moment the photos were taken: after making love, sated, the bedspread crumpled on the ground, F. posing a bit reluctantly, P. thrilled, with Pachuca or San Luis Potosí outside, fireworks cracking, celebrating some saint or other. M. felt dizzy at the sight. She'd never look like that; she'd never be so free. She sobbed. She wanted to tear up the photos. She returned them to their

envelope. She read L.'s letters with indifference; they were innocent as a schoolgirl's, tender, besotted.

Oh, my little pumpkin, I'm dying to see you.
Yesterday I saw my friend C. and told her all about
us, how well we understand each other, how much
you make me laugh. Do you still love me?

That's what most of them were like. Her friend C.
was a constant witness; L. was insecure, needed
permission for everything. She must have bored
P. In any case, M. resented her less. Even though
she was the most beautiful, the most perfect. Or
was she the woman in the photos?

She returned the letters to the drawer and
flopped down onto the bed. She didn't know
how she could go on.

That evening, she faked cheerfulness and
P. was happy to see her happy. The next night,
though, she started to dig. She made up a story
about how she'd come across the letters and
asked P., "Who are F. and A. and L.?" At first,
he refused to tell her. M. insisted. Her curiosity
must have flattered P.; eventually he relented
and told her about each woman with relish.
They joked. M. jeered. Then she told him that

the envelope of photos had fallen out and she couldn't not look at them. "Those are mine," P. protested. And they fought and M. cried and he stomped into the bedroom, opened the drawer, rummaged around for the envelope, took out the photos, and tore them up. "Is that what you wanted?" he yelled. M. tried to grab them away, to protect them as if they belonged to her too, but it was impossible. They ended up scattered all over the rug, and much later M. swept them up and threw them out.

"Isn't that horrible?"
"Awful."

No theory or conjecture can capture these examples and fully represent them. I guess jealousy is never abstract enough to fit a single definition. They burgeon into aphorisms, epigrams, short stories, novels: there are always more examples. I've found some lines in La Rochefoucauld that could serve as frontispieces:

"Jealousy is in a manner just and reasonable, as it tends to preserve a good which belongs, or which we believe belongs to us."

"There is more self-love than love in jealousy."

"Jealousy is the worst of all evils, yet the one that is least pitied by those who cause it."

"The cure for jealousy is certain knowledge of what we were afraid of, for it puts an end to life or love. It is a cruel remedy, but kinder than doubt and suspicions."

Anyone who can define jealousy probably isn't jealous. M. can't define it. When she talks about retrospective jealousy, no hypotheses come to mind, only memories. She asks if I've read *Before She Met Me*, a novel by Julian Barnes. The protagonist lives with his wife, an actress, and is deeply in love with her. One afternoon he goes to the movies alone. There's a series of shorts before the film, including snippets of old second-tier movies that never made it to theaters. Suddenly, he's presented with the enormous image of his wife kissing another man. The protagonist is as horrified as if he were watching the real thing, not a performance. From that moment onward, he's tortured by the past. He resolves to track down all of his wife's old movies and watch them and confront her. The outcome is violent.

M. has given up. Her jealousy exceeds the scope of her will, the machine of her convictions. When she imagines paradise, she imagines a gathering of indifferent souls. Her soul surveys human passions from on high and invents an apothegm: "Love is a shape made of three never-equidistant angles." And another: "Two always includes the promise of three." And then the modern, unprejudiced mind would see that jealousy is what exists before reason starts to meddle with appearances. Before examples.

9.

GOOD AND BAD

I'm not a good person. I discovered this a long time ago and recently, finally, admitted it. The admission must make me better, or at least that's my hope. It's been said and read in certain manuals that if you accept your limitations, you instantly transcend them. By acknowledging my not-goodness, maybe I'll become less bad as a result. Although the problem isn't really *badness*, which is somehow an active, complex attribute, but a kind of moral backwardness, inertia, fragmentation. As if I were always far removed from wherever things take place. As if the delay in their image distorted my judgment. As if the only response were a lack of response; omission over commission. As if life were something that happened to other people and you were condemned to observe it from afar, between simulation and postponement, considering what you'd do in their shoes—until the moral instinct is suffocated by the vanity of imagination and you're already responsible, even though you haven't lifted a finger.

Good and bad look like masks when you focus too hard on how they express their intentions. Demure, you stop, deducing the bias out of fear: the truth can't overcome the lie. It's a matter of words and fictions. I see ordinary, everyday goodness as a reward for learning to measure the scale of each passing day: x thing on Monday, y on Tuesday. And a suspension of caution on weekends, because pleasure has a dangerous way of tampering with our expectations. Other people's goodness surprises me because I tend to overlook it in search of blame. When I find it, I realize that the exegesis was excessive; the act was sacrificed to its interpretation. There's one last resort: the interminable review, Mr. Prufrock's "visions and revisions," marked less by wickedness than by constant hesitation. What face should I prepare? Which is presumptuous, because you don't know all the faces you make; only other people do. And the face of goodness, as nearly as I can tell, doesn't move much, doesn't alter its features to make room for fleeting emotions. The art of austerity rules supreme because its designs are simple. That's what I think I've perceived: not too many superimposed faces, but a single, stable face that looks back at me without casting even the slightest shadow.

My lived experience is limited; I'm more witness than participant. But I know many good people, I observe them with an almost pitiful admiration, and I try to figure out what goes on in their heads. My own mistrust helps me identify strategies, which I quickly discard when I see that their goodness has kicked in without any thought to the consequences, without even the benefit of recognition. I focus then on the goodness itself. Unfortunately, it's not transferrable, not even by demonstration. Good people intervene before they even know why. They're unconcerned with eking out a specific explanation. Searching for some trace of ambition, I stumble into the same face as before, smiling now. I think about regret and remember that there are no crossroads in goodness, just equal amounts of instinct and spontaneity. As if it transpired in a time before the person herself, or as if it didn't belong to the conscience or weren't an attribute, just a reflex.

What parameters can I possibly establish if I live on the other side? There are long stretches of silence in my head, with no openings to grant them an immediate presence. My inner world falls silent under the weight of thoughts or habits. Whereas I've noticed that good people are loquacious, deftly mastering the language of emotions. Sometimes I've wondered whether it's a kind of rhetoric, because one good person's discourse resembles another's. The question, of course, is built into my own failings. It has nothing to do with goodness itself, which must by nature be expressed in general terms. I know that good people start with a simple

formula of love for others and that this love doesn't fal-
ter in the careful, personal selection of sentences. When
it appears in literature (poetry is full of examples), my
obsession with analogies instantly interferes, and I start
to ferret around the verses for an exhibitionist morality. Meting out current events in a poem causes spatial
constraints: poetry comes fully furnished. It's a tacti-
cal challenge, making room for indignation or solidarity without the paintings falling off the walls, the rugs
ripping, the corners cracking. You have to find the convention or the code that works in every case. In poetry,
the language of goodness emerges from the premise that
the poet, the author, is an intrinsic part of the solution,
because she sensed the problem and can even solve it
melodically. Music makes me anxious: what do beauty
and harmony hide? I poke around the paraphernalia,
searching for the sensitive person's vanity: the kind that
feels for you, that speaks on your behalf. I home in on
the words, on the effect they cause when you hear them
and then when you read them to yourself. When I'm
alone with goodness, it totters like a clumsy puppet. I
don't yet know how to move the strings.

Maybe, in the depths of poetry, there's an incor-
ruptible kernel that no poem can compromise.
Goodness sits there quietly until the murmur chimes
in again and approval spreads like a slow, inextinguish-
able flame. Among people, though, it has other ways of

seeping in. I've seen individuals turned to fellow beings, then to a collective "us." I've longed to join the commotion. I've had few chances to cut into the current. My lack of goodness halts my momentum. In political discussions, I confuse victims with leaders and get hung up on the shouting from below: what happened to the first cry, the real one? In this country, crowds are instantaneous. And they gather out of curiosity, convenience, or even conviction. When I see photos in the newspaper the next day—the leader on his dais, surrounded by the latest multitude, hands in the air, open-mouthed—I start to categorize their attitudes. As if politics had to be sterilized to be plausible, as if the causes didn't precede the propaganda that deforms them. I wish I could sneak in before the show. If goodness exists, then it must live in the preparations, the fear, the landscape of dust and tin and iron they're advancing through, the collective I can't see head-on. They'll have names, like everyone else. They'll have complexities before they multiply. I'll examine the subterfuges with a detective's relish. And once again, my aspirations will evaporate. And once again, I'll wonder about the primitive mechanism of my incredulity. Who installed it in me without my permission?

I study myself carefully. Inside, I possess all the right intentions: I commiserate all day and every day, I'm enraged by injustice, I'm fed up with corruption, I hate bad policy, I'm terrified by violence, I share everyone else's wish for a better world. But goodness keeps eluding me as if I didn't deserve it. On a personal level, I haven't yet had to face large-scale crises—war, revolution, exile, hiding—or life-and-death decisions, so I have no idea how I would behave. As for electoral debacles, I've had a predictable range of reactions: from the euphoria I felt when I voted for the first time (at age thirty-six) to my disenchanted abstention in recent campaigns. On each occasion, I've heard good people admonish and browbeat me, and I've watched them resolutely support a particular candidate. Of each period, I recall the intensity, not the arguments. In recent wrathful years, my desire to think correctly has been thrown into disarray. I listen to the shouts, the slogans, the accusations, and the certainties, but I can't seem to get myself to the proper place, and so I'm left outside, examining cracks for keys to the mystery. Which is additional proof of my shortcomings: there is no mystery in goodness. There are causes. Ideally, you devote yourself to them. Through your own actions, wherever you can. Good people can quickly identify commitment and carry it out. They're the proprietors of outcomes and collective identifications.

I admire them again and again. I consider the points of view: the oblique and the headlong. I look for the heart. Which, according to Hannah Arendt, is a terrible political adviser: extravagant love for others conceals a thirst for power, for representativity. But those words and their speculative origins come apart in my mouth. Like parts of an old tool that's conventional enough to still work, and which I don't know how to use because I can't seem to fit them into a tradition of my own. The oblique gaze becomes a mockery of direct stares. For being gullible, simple, naive. Aesthetics rises above politics and judges it. When desperation interferes, good people's behavior feels like a hysterical play that never reaches catharsis. That's what the oblique gaze gets done. It condemns the means, not the content. The good people I know have a mission and won't sacrifice it in the name of form. As it should be, I say to myself, from the window overlooking the street.

Even so, my supply of goodness is limited. I don't see clearly in introspection; something essential is always hidden there. I find more hang-ups than personality. Maybe that's the problem. Goodness needs a way to channel its enthusiasm; a safe place to cleave the words of protest. Not this sediment, this obsession with artifice. Not this intimacy that takes too long to analyze the principles and insists that coherence is the only infallible one. Even if, in daydreams, it shines like someone eager to lavish the world with good deeds. Until it bumps into its latest fellow being, and gets tangled up in what's read between the lines, and abstains or freezes in place instead of being good. And then it loses its chance, because its fellow being was only passing through.

I know I'm bungling categories: confusing public morality with private, goodness with social and political habits. Maybe it all comes down to manners, to the particular ceremony of your interactions with others. I've always been frightened by the art of concealment, not because I'm overly frank but because I lack the resources to embellish my own absence. As I understand it, the unspoken rule is that you shouldn't say what you really think and no one should be able to tell what you really feel. The proper protocol involves detours and circumlocutions because the alternative would be unbearable. But then the relationship between truth and goodness warps. Being good means adhering to a set of conventions and leaving the chaff to intimacy, which chews at it, processes it slowly, and never discards it altogether. Inside is invisible from outside. Every mind is a world, as the saying goes, which upsets the stability of paranoid reason—which in turn fears becoming the cause of every breach.

The lesson is simple: goodness can mean the constant declaration of feelings and intentions. In the long run, discursive vertigo becomes a profession of faith. I've seen it take center stage and run the show; I've seen the message get mistaken for the messenger. I've heard good people voice their distress: are we just going to keep doing nothing in the face of all this horror? I'm tempted by goodness; I'm tempted to belong. Some years ago, a good person accused me of being a reactionary because I questioned a politician's motives. My first instinct was to apologize, but good people see beyond the bones, I realized in time; they understand that such mistakes reveal irreversible ideological damage. According to Czeslaw Milosz, "To belong to the masses is the great longing of the 'alienated intellectual.'" I'm not an intellectual, but I'm afraid I'm certainly alienated. Good people don't shrink from collective passions. The excitement of putting myself at the service of a cause excites me until the cause gets extroverted and uses words that crumble inside me because I've never heard them in my head before, never thought them in first person: if I don't think them, they don't think me. That's how puritanical my idiosyncrasy has become.

The verdict is as vast as the guilt. I follow good people closely and don't care about the anomalous details that can sprout up in intimate conversation. My starting point is my own moral poverty, the perspective that makes everything else look fanatical. At social gatherings, I'm alarmed by my inability to exclaim when I'm supposed to, my incapacity to stifle sarcasm, no matter how on point it may be. Melodramatically, I'd clarify: I'm not bad, I just turn out to be no one when it's time to step out of myself. A rag doll with its dress on backward, making the flower print look like misshapen stains. My fellow being is troubled by the sight. As far as just causes are concerned, I find it astonishing that the defender often progresses, but the cause rarely does. Although I'm jumbling my categories again. In every-day life, good people always put me in my place. Which isn't a hole, but an edge: there, I blend in with all the other witnesses who still can't prepare a face to meet the faces that we meet. If there were anything mystical about passivity, I'd join good people without any kind of permission stepping in to mediate. And I'd do the obvious thing: I'd imitate them. Until any sign of simulation had been erased.

10.

IN DEFENSE OF PESSIMISM

The major obstacle for pessimism, it seems to me, is that it has to oppose optimism. In this constant opposition, it becomes so monotonous that it risks persuading its followers to switch sides. Personally, I'm disconcerted by people who always put a cheerful face on things, who make the best out of even the most terrible circumstances, who insist that something was good when it was obviously bad. But I worry that pessimism—or, better put, the expression of pessimism—is even more dismaying. It's boring, repetitive, and overblown. Besides, we have to admit that any campaign for an unequivocal No has a backdrop of optimism: it wants to be right, to win the match. A pessimist sometimes commits the sin of naiveté, of self-absorption. She fails to notice that her melancholy, her resignation, her grim outlook, have become a demagogy of promises; if kept, they threaten to make her happier, or at least bring her some satisfaction. She succumbs, then, to a paradox: to a perverse optimism. The only way out is silence. A true pessimist explains nothing, leaving the virtues and banalities of eloquence to the optimist.

I didn't mean to start out by criticizing pessimism. In fact, as my title implies, I wanted to do exactly the opposite. But in the interests of documenting and strengthening my negative argument, I decided to consult an author who was popular in the eighties and maybe early nineties: E. M. Cioran. I thought his work would offer me the purest distillation of an epigrammatic, sardonic intelligence; that every sentence would flesh out a mood beyond any particular experience, good or bad. I imagined a keen, penetrating lucidity, something in the vein of Chamfort or Lichtenberg, but already adapted to a new set of rules. In short, I committed the great pessimist sin: I expected something. I didn't have a tool as drastic as outdatedness at my disposal. Cioran's melodramatic delirium belonged to another era; mine, if not the world's. I remember several of my friends reading this Romanian-in-Paris as the great messenger of a hope-drained apocalypse. A dystopia where you could hate and lob insults in style, where you could cultivate a fascination with death without stooping to the vulgarity of dying. Even suicide was on the side of the believers, of the optimists. Cioran taught you that a lack of resources, procedures, systems led to a sole unobjectionable truth: our life in this world is meaningless and we're here by accident. Any sort of ontology or theology you try to build on this foundation is a purely theatrical gesture. At the end of the day, we're going to die, and one thing will replace another. "I believe in the future of the terrible," wrote Cioran. The line is as powerful as a joke. If you don't laugh, it means you prefer happiness.

Cioran arrived in Paris in 1937 and spent the next twenty-eight years living in a hotel on the Rive Gauche before he finally moved into a small apartment. Not having a house, furniture, or (especially) a library was a key part of his advocacy for disillusionment. He whiled away the days in a room, in university restaurants, and on walks around the city and the Luxembourg Gardens. A perennial insomniac, he often wandered and took notes at night. Boredom was the wellspring of his vision. So his own life had begun: "I could pinpoint the exact moment of my first fit of boredom, at the age of five. But what for? I have always been enormously bored." He wrote his first book, *On the Heights of Despair*, in 1934, at the age of twenty-two. Amazingly, he didn't change his mind or mood until his death in 1995. What's interesting, though, is that he insisted on writing at all, on communicating something that denied the importance of communication. I read six of Cioran's books. Except for *Exercises in Admiration*, a selection from his *Notebooks* (published posthumously), and *Conversations*, I always felt as if I were reading the same book. His exercises and aphorisms were marked by recurring themes:

ennui, the absence of God, intrinsic and peripheral Nothingness, suffering as a nearly hygienic activity, the uselessness and deceitfulness of traditional philosophy, the stupidity of glory and humanity, the inefficacy of love, the exaltation of death, and the fear of dying. At first, this repetitiveness suggests a system of thought. Later, though, once you've got enough pages behind you, it feels more like sterility, like glamorized poverty. There's also something dissonant about Cioran's desolation: a poetic, lyrical, romantic tone that brings him dangerously close to the sentimentalism he snubbed. It seems that he had a stronger literary vocation than a philosophical one, but there was only enough of both talent and premises to destroy the principle of their imagined construction. Cioran himself admitted in his *Notebooks* that he was a sentimental man, an old-school romantic. He even tried to justify the patent sterility of his best-known work: "During the time when I wrote in the first person, everything came out on its own: ever since I buried the 'I,' even the merest phrase demands effort and I feel no inclination to produce it. Impersonality paralyzes my spontaneity." Perhaps as a result of editorial pressure following his relative success (he won several prizes, though he accepted only the first), Cioran became an expert in bad omens and worse news. Very much in spite of himself, as is clear in his *Notebooks*. There we can see the full drama of an oeuvre composed entirely of disjointed remarks; we can appreciate its tragic incongruity, its utter authenticity. That's the other side, dark and realist, of Cioran: a writer who comes off as a mere speaker even in his most famous books, a publicist trained in the nuances of horror. There, too, is the whole argument behind his indifference: Cioran truly didn't care what became of his work. It was just an instrument he honed to mitigate the vastness of time. Writing poems may have been his dearest wish; his words often skirt that void. He was mortified by the beauty of the sky or the sea or a bluff in winter. In prose, his immediacy crumbled and exposed the fundamental dilemma of transient things: only a poem could have successfully captured the fleeting instant of joy and communion.

There are no loose ends in Cioran. Any objection you might take to his work will appear and be rationally addressed in his *Notebooks* and interviews. When asked in 1977 why he bothered writing if he found it so futile and laborious, he said: "Because writing, however little, has helped me pass from one year to the next, the expressed obsessions being weakened and—halfway—overcome. To produce is an extraordinary comfort. And to publish, another." He stressed in the same interview that he didn't care about the reader at all; he wrote only to cure himself of his disturbances. The fragmentary nature of his work also obeyed a protocol of pain, even freedom. Philosophy was possible only as shard, as splinter, as explosion. That was Nietzsche's great lesson, his proof of honesty, of fidelity to the unstable essence of thought. When you start a long essay, Cioran said, you start with a series of assertions, generalizations, and then you end up "their prisoner. A certain sense of honor obliges you to keep respecting them until the end, to not contradict yourself . . . This is the drama of all structured thought, refusing contradiction . . . By contrast, if you write in fragments, you can say one thing and its opposite within the span of a single day." In Cioran, this positive contradiction is barely perceptible, maybe because he's less interested in ideas than in what happens when you erase them. Ideas impeded the atmosphere he liked surviving in: nothingness, the void, words that now sound like frumpy garments, but which Cioran had perfected through everyday faith. Commemorating failure, describing it (albeit with such literary flair that it seemed suspicious), was among his major goals. If he happened to bump into readers and admirers as he performed this feat, that was an accident; it never moved Cioran to redeem his unjust cause and decamp to the side of human warmth and happiness.

Unsettlingly, Cioran's best work isn't his most deliberately philosophical books, but the justifications he laid out in his *Notebooks* and declared in interviews. There, we find a fully realized, self-directed sarcasm, a swift and marginal skepticism, without the ideology and concealment he inflicted on his most orthodox tracts. Fragmentariness didn't release him from the yoke of repetition, nor from the burden of assembling a contrary system. Cioran was imprisoned by a freedom that ossified into a formula and a style that kept him from inventing new ones. What he wanted to say was unilateral in the end; it had no internal contradictions. Contradictions existed outside, in life itself, where Cioran came and went as a mere person with friends, social commitments, lovers, appointments, conversations, and probably long stretches of normalcy.

According to Cioran, style was a tether that limited him when he adopted the French language. Before, he'd written in Romanian, a language lighter in academic and literary tradition, malleable enough to allow him a greater range of movement. He could write poorly without worrying about reception. In French, he became more conscious and therefore less confident. He donned a mask and altered his entire fate, in a way. Fortunately, he managed to integrate this metamorphosis into his general fatalism: a language was at fault for its constrictions, not its content.

I see little difference between the books translated from Romanian and those translated from French. The ones he wrote in his first language may be a little harsher, a little more bombastic. Cioran learned certain

rituals of courtesy; in any case, he met some of its inter-
locutors and learned to write with them breathing down
his neck. No matter what, it's odd that a negative message should become so popular, that a dream of solitude
should prompt a collective aspiration. Cioran confessed
that most of his readers were crazy, potentially suicidal;
people who saw him less as an author than as a therapist
of darkness. He also confessed that he'd put "the worst
of myself" into his books. Whether or not he provoked
it, maybe he deserves the revenge of our indifference.
But what he awakens in the long run, when you start to
see the message as a never-ending story, is an ennui and
an irritation much like what he experienced himself. A
certain intellectual distrust, we could say, if we wanted
to be pompous about it. As if Cioran had taken the easy
way out: destroying everything, then mocking the ridic-
ulousness of the wreckage. In another interview, he said
that his penchant for fragments and aphorisms was the
result of laziness. To write whole texts, one had "to be
an active person . . . I was born in the fragment." Which
oscillates between enigma and a historical (nearly hysterical) description of Romania.

Regret may be the dark side of pessimism. Cioran
was guilty of having vehemently supported the Iron
Guard in his country, and of having admired Hitler and
Nazism during his two-year stint in Germany. In a text
dated July 15, 1934, he wrote: "There is no politician

today who inspires me with greater sympathy and admiration than Hitler." While Cioran recognized the Führer's monstrosity, he believed that only someone like him could lead a nation to greatness. He even wrote a book on the subject, *The Transfiguration of Romania*, which shamed him for the rest of his life. Beset by Alzheimer's, he authorized a new edition in Romania, never in France.

His followers barely dwell on these disgraces, or else they write them off as youthful sins. For example, in the Spanish-language edition published by Tusquets as *Conversaciones*, a timeline makes only fleeting mention of his sympathy for the Iron Guard, which it further downplays by remarking on his mystical explorations. It says nothing at all about his fascination with Hitler. In 1986, a journalist from *Die Zeit* asked Cioran about his fascist youth. Deft as ever, he responded: "It wasn't their ideas that interested me, just their enthusiasm. It established a kind of bond between those people and me. A pathological story, at the end of the day. Because, in my culture and my conceptions, I was completely different from them." In France, he tried to expunge all evidence of these low passions and became fanatically apolitical. To an extent, his furious pessimism was a veiled rationalization of his youthful bedazzlements: if nothing matters, then bad things don't matter, either. The final consequence of such a paradigm is an uncomfortable if elegant frivolity. That's where Cioran planted himself to lob his invectives.

His work shows a surprising reverence for enthusiasm: a kind of spirited rage that ultimately comes off as intense engagement. Cioran took great pleasure in his boundless discursive capacity, which was rooted in total denial. On this foundation, he could build absolutely anything. He claimed he wasn't pessimistic, but merciful: "Even 'consoling.' I'm a modest benefactor. But my remedy isn't universal." Still, it's a remedy, which points to a kind of hope, and to the very key to pessimism as a strategy or superstition. If you adopt an absolutely negative view of the world, whatever life brings you, even the most ordinary life, will mark so great a difference that it will grant you, bearer of pessimism, a middling happiness. The knot's complexity doesn't weaken it. Words are the tricky part: writing down what should only be insinuated as prophecy, if you're pretentious, or as prediction, if you're pragmatic. The major flaw of pessimism may be that it leaves no room for exceptions or for changing your mind. If you're a pessimist, you can't just declare that you're going to be optimistic for a while. Although your twisted nature may argue that you may as well be happy, since nothing matters in the first place. But then you'd renounce the petty power of always auguring a dismal outcome. These are the weapons of a demiurge who never misses a shot: if the bad things you predicted don't come to pass, your relief is almost happiness. If your prediction is fulfilled, you're delighted to have been right, and tolerably proud. You had the last word, the famous "I told you so": a comforting slogan that, among other things, erases any inkling of chance.

Cioran grew tired of "defaming the universe." After many books and an ambiguous celebrity, he resolved to keep quiet. But it may have been too late. His pessimism had already calcified into a school and brought him considerable fortune. Is there anything that unnerves disenchantment more than becoming its mouthpiece? Such a gloomy outlook could easily have ended in suicide, or at least insanity, not the salons and magazines of Paris. Ever astute, Cioran turned both exits into maxims: suicide in its most positive portrayal ("It's very important to know that we can kill ourselves whenever we want. That calms us, it satisfies us. The problem is solved and the comedy continues") and madness as a special effect of intensity, the gizmo of a mind already used to tussling with monsters. Near the end of his life, he agreed that his role as a source of moral support, as a secular confessor, was hugely ironic: "Surviving a destructive book is always painful for a writer." Even his own pessimism let him down. Cioran failed to attain the failure he had so vehemently foretold. He even achieved his goal of never working: he lived off the generosity of several patrons and then off the employment of his wife, Simone Boué. Faced with such ambivalent triumphs, he found a palliative measure: becoming disappointed with disappointment, then shutting up. The aging, ailing body would see to the rest.

For consistency's sake, a pessimist must have bad luck. Otherwise, at least a bit of optimism would be in order. Any flaws in a pessimist's mechanical addiction to devastating prognoses don't prove her wrong; they only postpone the consequences. There are many conventional days between one thunderous aftereffect and another. And it's there, in these spells of painless duration, that pessimism acts as a modulating instrument, a method of contrast, administering modest doses of well-being. The game depends on how you treat the throw of the dice: is it the premise or the conclusion? Depending on how the pieces fall, you—a pessimist—can mold misfortune to the circumstances and cause occasional sparks of happiness. The trick is to never believe they'll ever happen again. It's less a decision than a kind of artisanal conjecture. It's something you do in deference to tradition, or because it's in your nature, not because you really know anything.

In the end, it's still a cage. Schopenhauer became famous in part for his insults and negativity, not his philosophy alone. People wanted to revel in his brouhaha from up close, like a circus animal, and hear him proclaim those terrible truths out loud: "For whence did

Dante get the material for his hell, if not from this actual world of ours?" Life swung between the "two foes" of "pain and boredom"; no pleasure was powerful enough to disrupt the perfect, immutable measure of suffering. Like Voltaire's Candide, the optimist would say that this is the best of all possible worlds, no matter what; we should learn to relativize before imposing our limits. Such mediocrity would make a pessimist laugh. The real, whole truth can't depend on something as volatile as perspective. Human life, Schopenhauer concluded, is "a natural history of pain, which is summarized as follows: want without reason, always suffer, [fight continuously], and then die . . . And so on for centuries upon centuries until our planet is torn to pieces."

On a personal level, it's a question of temper: the pessimist's bad mood, the optimist's good one. Which you don't get to choose. You adapt, learn, or unlearn, and that's it. Unfortunately, no attitude can change the fundamental fact of death. The forward path is all we've got. The optimist knows how to maneuver; the pessimist, like a fanatical dog, won't drop the bone of obviousness. This makes pessimism a harder position to defend. Sometimes, on slightly brighter days, the pessimist catches a glimpse—between the lines, or behind bars—of her opposite. And then she realizes that they've always been together. And the danger, the danger of discord, lifts her spirits.

11.

MY OTHER *ISMS*

ABYSS(ISM)

It was fashionable to hover at the edges of abstract abysses (cerebral ones, of course) in the late 1970s and early 1980s. I did it. My intense, subjugated readings of Blanchot, Bataille, Klossowski, Deleuze, Foucault, Derrida, and some Bachelard (the most romantic of the lot) prompted me to pursue the famous *mise en abyme* and some no less illustrious "limit-experiences." To create the proper atmosphere, you had to kindle a particular kind of sorrow, somewhere between philosophical and ideological; a disorientation that would undermine the direct meaning, the innocent meaning, of language. Clear expression was suspect, because clarity endorsed the orthodoxy of significances—and of surfaces, which was even worse. You had to sink into a textual, parenthetical silence if you wanted to be spared the danger of misunderstandings. You also had to dominate exquisite dialectics between equals (the writing of writing, the reason of reason, the visibility of the visible) and take deft detours into inextricable opposites: the absence of presence, the knowledge of unknowing, the sense of senselessness. You had to repeat terms like "immanence," "rupture," "discursivity," and "negation" as if they were the very formulae of a prayer. Those of us with a knack for it could recognize each other in how perfectly we operated this solipsistic terminology. In the end, you sank into an abyss yourself.

I had a private tutor in the subject of chasms and their edges. He was from Guadalajara, he smoked cigars, and he'd had a French lover, Nadine or Anouk. He listened to Rachmaninoff and wept when he pondered the Soviet Revolution and the fate of the proletariat. At critical moments, when I found myself moved by a passage in some novel or poem, he'd quote Lukács and remind me that all literature had a duplicitous bent. Sometimes he'd wait for me outside the philosophy department at the UNAM with a cigar and a copy of Blanchot or Deleuze tucked under his arm. He usually also had a flask of rum. One afternoon, we left the campus together and made our way up Insurgentes on foot. An emaciated dog sniffed around the sidewalk ahead of us. My tutor *en abyme* started to threaten it, trying to force it off the curb; he wanted to drive it into the roar of traffic. I begged him to stop. The dog whimpered in terror. My friend goaded it, charged it. The cars swerved and screeched around the dog until one struck it head-on. I screamed bloody murder. My friend and tutor tried to explain something about the mysticism of pain, the need to purge your feelings in preparation for the abyss of all abysses. I never saw him again. Later I heard that he'd joined the PRI.[2] In the end, it was a profoundly Mexican story.

ACTIVISM

Some years ago, in a Coyoacán café, a renowned activist spat at me, "So what have *you* done for the country?" I didn't answer. First, because her demand struck me as hysterical. And second, because my response would have been a confession: I haven't done anything for my country other than living in it. This sometimes troubles me: I may be passive, but I'm not indifferent. I read newspapers every day and follow the latest scandals. I discuss the news, support some accounts, reject others. As I doze off at night, as the fledgling images of my dreams clumsily cohere, certain events return to mind: bodies in a mass grave, declarations by the candidate du jour, open mouths at a rally. The public forum of the living and the dead causes me such vertigo that I try to focus on the figures, or on the language that explains them, or both. I

---

2. The autocratic political party that ruled Mexico for over seventy years.

fall asleep when my consciousness scuttles away through a shortcut and the repetitive mechanism of reflection switches off at last. But this routine certainly doesn't amount to "doing something for the country."

I've gone to a few rallies lately. As usual, my conviction or morbid curiosity dwindles en route. I have to go if I'm going to come back, I tell myself, or I'm told by the fable of my own eternal return. On the way, I distract myself at street stalls, stop to peer into store windows, drag my feet, and still invariably show up ahead of schedule, which bewilders me; my tardiness, I sense, reveals a certain desperation for a life I'll never truly live. Today, I think, maybe I'll jump from the sidelines into the center. And I lean against a wall with my body as a fortress.

At the meeting place, some ten activists are milling around the esplanade with caps and signs. They look me over. They're professional demonstrators, the real thing. I pretend I've ended up there by accident. They share a set of paraphernalia: a little flag, a whistle, a handful of ribbons, a walking stick. They have backpacks and newspapers. Gradually, friends and acquaintances appear. I join the growing crowd as we recognize each other, greeting each other with glimmers of goodwill: we're here out of solidarity, ready to take to the streets. There's pride in it, but reticence, too. It's not because of us, contemplative beings that we are, but because of the brutality, the horror, that we've resolved to join the protest this afternoon. We exchange jokes and contact info as we wait for things to start. Heading the throng are leaders with megaphones I never see. Someone gives orders. Suddenly the crowd shifts into formation and starts moving toward the Zócalo. I hear shouts and slogans, tics of memory that organize into a collective yell and then dissolve into silence. People march; from the sidewalk, other people watch them march. I'm excited by this simultaneity: It's the country, I tell myself, and I'm inside it.

In the Zócalo, the crowd turns a corner toward the church called the Sagrario Metropolitano, where the bandstand is. People arrange themselves around it, ready to listen. Little by little, against my will, I feel my energy draining into the abstract speeches, the pep talks, the exalted metaphors of pain and altruism. As if things didn't happen but simply repeated themselves. Yet this aesthetic assessment—I scold myself again— ignores the immediate, existential power of the march, which my frivolous stylistic fixation prevents me from really registering. From the dais, a speaker declares that history and the working class will witness a blow to the fascist regime disguised as democracy. I close my eyes and focus on the irony spreading like uncomfortable flames: there could be another body in the rubble. And then, once again, I don't do anything for my country.

(Note: One Sunday afternoon in May, on the sidewalk, with the acid heat pressing down on the crowd, I glimpsed the birth of a new leader, a new saint of civic life. "There he is!" the voices said. "Here he comes!" I glimpsed his hand and hat and thought of the idols fabricated and then felled by admiration. And I apologized to him right away, new and afflicted as he was.)

LYRICISM

A. It's a special effect or a traditional affect. An empty pool still bright with the water's reflections. A stretch of dry grass and a bit of mud tugging the blades toward the sanity of pavement. A morning before or a night after the declaration of love for one's fellow beings. An analogy between the mutilated body and the barbs reaching into the garden. A pulpit where the voice cracks and quavers with its truth. A secular pretext or teleological leak. A biography on behalf of others or a feeble person in the corner of a house, fingers greased with red or yellow paint, face flickering with fear or exasperation. No blood on the stairs. No old moss or certain trace or path or dissenting ins and outs.

I peer through the glass to take in the details: lichen, frost, seas, foam unfurling like a white line before dissolving into the bricks in a wall; milk from stones or loose sap before the tires screech around the curve and a certain kind of patience dies with it.

What's it about?

I didn't reach out any hands yesterday, or turn the other cheek, or love my neighbors when they demanded a cordial, civic truce, or at least my silence amid the red tape of borders and syllables enmeshed with the ardent campaign of the *spirit*. I didn't clear the road so the green shoots could be cut or the drills be cleaved in the gravel strip I walk across, listening for my shoes' most distracted echo. I didn't want to see the solemn man with his clipboard of figures who rang my buzzer and clanged a broken bell at midday. I didn't leave my plush gray skull, the upside-down image with its discordant *corrido:* *"Bring your pussy to the tip and I'll eat you out, use your tongue and lips or I'll hit you, pretty girl . . ."*

Yesterday I was told in code that there would be "whales." Then the man of corners and parapets would save us all. "All of us?" And my colleague nodded with a wink sealed off from the sun.

A minute of his time is a second of my own. Outside, amid the gates and grates and tin sheets, the crime has already been committed. What was going to happen has happened. And it's a dog's life to end up living somewhere with no one. And it's a cat's life to test your skin when lyricism shinnies up us like a reptile in complicity with the shape of the ritual that instantly turns into a public square so the pious can recite their list of verses, eyes welling with enormous, tender tears.

Say proclaiming your feelings isn't enough. Or the delirium of names isn't enough.

When the figure of the crime approaches with its attentive damsel and dirty crinoline, I'll say I'm not home. And if it shows up singing, I'll take off at a tangent.

So: *what's it about?*

B. *I'm unfamiliar with the terms of the debate.*
Is that how you say it? Or how do you say it? Worse yet, how do you spell it? The debate on what's happening outside?

It might be timidly suggested that colossal acts are winning, for now, in every sense, over words.

It rings hollow.

Or that poetry (Mexican poetry being the implicit context here) must learn many lessons in harsh realism to be cured, finally, of its landscapist, decorative, static, ahistorical, superfluous inertia.

That sounds better, more conclusive. The next question is who has the authority to deliver the instructions.

The noise begins.

C. I'm looking when I should be listening. The podiums multiply. Two ancient schools; the engaged poets and the *poetic* poets, detached, exquisite (effeminate, as they would have been disparaged in the age of José Vasconcelos[3]). And our circumstances? Marked, usually, by sweet and expedient state subsidies.

Someone asks me: "Are you left-wing or right-wing? You have to define yourself . . ." But the question, in my case, isn't valid anymore. Both sides boast of having erased the entryways. The threat is imminent.

What is that?

A subverted Eden and its screechy bolt.[4]

Some tell me they don't know how to handle lyricism: from above or from below. Appropriating other

---

3. A Mexican writer, philosopher, and politician whose theories on *mestizaje* and institutional leadership (as the rector of the National Autonomous University of Mexico, the head of the Secretary of Public Education, etc.) had a powerful influence on the development of modern Mexico.
4. A line from Ramón López Velarde, Mexico's "national" poet par excellence—and one of Mexico's greatest poets in any era.

people's pain to cultivate poems that depict them, the poets, as kindhearted souls? Or subsumed in the usual Arcadia, with its orchard of dry leaves and narrow rivers? There, the narcotic eyelid[5] simulates tiny constellations when the eyes find a hiatus and people leap to shelter on steady ground. Holding on to each other.

D. We could state the obvious in its many forms: lyricism is subterfuge; lyricism is a peaceful place where our voices reconcile, modulating beautiful, insignificant verses; lyricism is the oracle we deliberately ignore in the chambers of poetry; I am lyricism, speaking for you and for them with interlinked similes and a god at the end of the stanza to enable our transcendence; I am lyricism, you are lyricism in a room, laboriously composing works in that storied genre: window poems.

Then what. The accusations will come. You can already hear them: "What about reality? Cowards!"

5. López Velarde again.

MYSTICISM

In certain lush gardens or in the middle of nature, staring out at a mountain range or a forest or a torrid river or a still pond, I've sensed gods, followed by an overwhelming urge to commune with their advent. The trance lasts for just a few moments. Thus far, I've never witnessed any presence that could be described as even remotely divine. At most, a breeze or sunbeam has shaped the sensuality of my perception, made me hunger for the nearness of another body. Once restored to myself, I'm flooded with a kind of shame. And the garden or the landscape recovers its usual opacity and I confine myself to a vacillation I'll call consciousness, for the sake of streamlining the paperwork.

I guess this trance must be an elemental form of mysticism. It only happens outdoors. Inside, with a roof over my head, I struggle to imagine such nostalgia: objects get in the way, furniture, paintings, all arranged with human intent. And I say nostalgia because the intuition feels like memory. As if I missed something I once possessed, deities or fictions or fables, and I were suddenly assailed by their absence in the relative anonymity of the natural world. To a religious person, this might be sufficient proof of divine existence. To me (agnostic and, worse yet, unbaptized), it's like a primitive reflex that instantly awakens when my own ignorance (confronted with the vast variety of trees, birds, insects, the impulse of a waterfall, etc.) admits defeat by the exacting individual design of the mystery. It feels that something sacred is still left in this world and it lets itself be pulled along until the weight of personhood interferes with the vision and any possible gods vanish into thin air.

In a now distant time, I tried to believe in god (the Catholic one). I even planned to be baptized and to finally take a proper name and join the community of my friends, who went to mass on Sundays and knew how to pray and cross themselves. I liked the ceremonies and the moral certitudes, the calendar-imposed obligations, the cross on people's foreheads on Ash Wednesday. My friends were in contact with something previous to them, situating them in a cultural dominion that excluded me. I assigned myself tasks. On certain days of certain months, I focused on making space for faith in my head, but I never managed to keep it open. I invented a rudimentary prayer and recited it before I went to sleep, kneeling beside my bed, but my own whisper in the darkness sounded ominous and I hid under the covers until my fear had melted away. I'd argued with my friends about the existence of god, wanting them to persuade me, but the subject didn't seem to trouble them; they didn't see it as a subject at all, just a deep faith they weren't getting rid of on my account. And they'd turn up the music or change the channel or the station and their silence contained centuries of history and tradition and mine contained scraps of language and vicious circles that tangled up with paradoxes or superstitions.

In the end, I gave up, vanquished by my obvious lack of vocation. I became agnostic in defiance of my father's furious atheism and to keep from further darkening the dark. My panic over my own meager piousness had predisposed me toward headlong lurches from one alternative to another, and there was something soothing about the anguish, as if it already meant an act of contrition, a plea for mercy. Besides, one advantage of indecisiveness was that I wouldn't miss out on either of two hypothetical outcomes: one with god and the other without (where I already lived on a daily basis). If Judgment Day ever came, I was sure that my discreet campaign in favor of the unknown would exonerate me even from limbo. If I'm not mistaken, doubt isn't a sin in the official kingdom of theology, and I've wrangled with most of my speculations at the feet of its pedestals. There aren't yet any saints or martyrs in the modest offerings I've assembled to scare off ghosts, but I know I can always change my mind and embrace a stricter sort of god. Alone, of course. And inside. Outside, I'd have to deal with the more pagan mysticism that seizes me whenever I take on a multiple identity. Like that of a tiny creature in the middle of the universe that doesn't know why it's here or what anything is for, other than contemplating the presences that something or someone has set before me to learn about or recognize.

SKEPTICISM

I don't know why those who worship the vice of uncertainty (myself among them) take pleasure in practicing it. All it does is condemn them to loneliness and melancholy, especially when reality gets darker and harsher than any certainty or act of faith that skeptics try to disprove with irony or doubt.

In my canonical, cobbled-together definition, skeptics reject all decision-making standards and insist, sometimes dogmatically, that we must observe, not assert. They see themselves as witnesses. Instinctively or pedantically, they mistrust all manner of interpretations, convictions, and conclusions. Devil's advocates or merely snobs, they always stand on the opposite shore of an emphasis. Silent on the razor's edge, they defend the perennial prudence of never having an opinion. "Why do you think what you think?" they ask with a faint, almost condescending smile. They evoke Socrates. They glimpse danger. They assume that their interlocutor will be patient enough to let them neatly and serenely unspool their arguments. But that's not usually the way it happens; the interlocutor is convinced of her truth. She lives inside it, and she views it in highly personal terms: it's hers, and she's going to defend it against every corrosive maneuver by the skeptics who, in a committed interlocutor's eyes, are victims of self-ishness, the bitterness of formal inquiry. Poor unscrupulous creatures you should treat with a trace of pity before you turn your back on them.

Unfortunately, real life doesn't grind to a halt as it does in Socratic dialogues, where skeptics and their interlocutor can talk and interrogations can flow into a single possible outcome: agreement, concord in difference. The result would be a strange sense of authority (the authority of suspended judgment) and an ensuing awkwardness: the skeptics would want their parcel of power, too, the realm of their inadequate reason. Before such an incongruity can take root, the finicky, solitary skeptics would rather keep ruminating on the elegance of their explanations, the richness of their nuances. Contemplating their efforts to expose every last angle of an argument, they mournfully accept their misfortune: their interlocutor, activist of her own mind, set them down on the side of the enemies, the adversaries with whom the skeptics will never agree. And then she left. When it comes to defining skepticism, I identify with its most unstable shadows. I'd have to doubt myself, too, tenuous even in darkness. But skepticism fractures my temperament, like a faulty machine asserting itself out of inertia, arguing just to prove it has a skeleton. If I believed in something, I'd avoid the traps of words altogether. A midafternoon slogan, a protested howl, a poem recited before a fervent audience return me to the business of politics. Where can you take a class in collective indignation?

A solidarity-minded friend admonishes or accuses me, depending on the size of my fault. I struggle to join her zeal. It must be because of the ideologue dressed up as a middle-aged man at a podium who speaks through her, or at least that's what I tell myself to neutralize my anxiety. If I yielded to enthusiasm, I'd become a follower, I'd be with the collective or some leader or official, I see myself offering my support, my symbolic hand, without any interfering introspection, because what's the point of questioning anything if everyone outside has the same opinion? The devil's tiny voice is shrill and interrupts us. When my friend outlines the horizon of peace and justice, my devil intervenes, slings the body on the table, and fishes around the scraps of flesh still clinging to its bones.

True skeptics shouldn't mock or fluster at other people's beliefs. And so my shoddy self will have to huddle in its hiding place, carefully rereading the manual on the proper practices of skepticism in times of war, violence, confusion, corruption, degradation, political intrigue, numerous leaders, their quota of devotees, and two or three caudillos.

12.

A CHRONICLE OF COMPASSION

1

It's a Saturday in a small town in Mexico. We've been reading poems to a solemn audience of exactly two people, whose applause thundered like a stadium's. Relative success trails us like a skittish cloud and we decide to go out into the bustling square for a cigarette. There are four of us. We're standing by the front door of the gallery where we read. We light our cigarettes and start ironizing about the reception of poetry (ours, at least) in pleasant little towns, but we're interrupted repeatedly by beggars, mostly women and children. I note that all four of us obey the same rules. The first time, we address the people who approach us: "Sorry, I don't have any change." The second, we shake our heads, half closing our eyes. And the third, we ignore them, hoping they'll desist and disappear. The rules are instinctive by now, hardwired into the identity of all Mexicans of any affluence, and it doesn't even curb our enthusiastic chatter to exercise them. In the end, the panhandlers come and go, and you never end up saying no to the same person. We've learned to coexist with poverty on an intimate and everyday basis. We're not indifferent, but we know the solution is beyond us. At most, we offer a little charity, a few spare coins, but we're not always up for it. Today is one of those days. There are so many people begging in the square that it's not enough to give to just one. We keep talking.

I say something to the others about the strangeness of our habits. They're not just strange: from a certain perspective, the most literal one, they're monstrous. When and how did we learn these rules? The four of us laugh nervously. The subject tends to manifest itself so ideologically (or hysterically) that it's better to subvert it with silence. What can poetry do? To compensate for their unease, some Mexican poets have incorporated poverty into their texts, like the garments of a keen social conscience, details that signal a lyrical form of engagement. Yet their actual affiliation with real-life poverty is in name only. The people in this plaza, thronging us now, are the canonical content, the quota of any experience on the streets of our country. Perhaps that's why we so easily group them together and avoid them. They'll always be there, beyond the walls of our houses and working spaces. And the rules, I suppose, help us bear this fact, help us accept our privilege with resignation, even indifference, without feeling directly responsible or ashamed.

In elemental and puritanical terms, it's worth acknowledging that there's something anomalous, warped, in the armature of our middle-class social education. What we've learned eats away at our placid image of normalcy. Which doesn't matter very much in the end: at some point in our lives, circumstances bear more weight than principles, and we all end up taking advantage of what comes with the whole package of that poverty. And we adapt. And some of us write poems about disaster again, condemn injustice, simplify messages, versify slogans, and sacrifice the metaphorical labyrinth for the sake of solidarity. And we feel at peace, because we trust we've helped lessen the blow of catastrophe. Responding to beggars is the least of it: they're contextual, and our indignation organizes itself around words, not faces. Given an audience, even if there are only two people in it, we'll know exactly how to commiserate; we'll deftly express our discontent. After the fact, word will get out: this poet feels the pain of brutal reality. And when you're driving your car or sitting on the terrace of some restaurant or standing on some corner, waiting for someone or something to arrive, the latest person will approach with their hand outstretched and you, exhausted, will apply the second rule, shaking your head no.

2

Inside, there are shortcuts for indulgence or theories that can help you sidestep social grief. Back in the seventies, I had a Trotskyite friend who would scold me whenever I gave spare change to a panhandler; "The revolution will never happen that way," he'd insist. Today's streets may still be walked by the children of that beggar, who didn't so much as glance at my friend. His own argument—that one-time charity is an obstacle to collective salvation—offered him a convenient and perpetual reprieve.

I'm always tangled up in virtues and emotions. I don't live in the long term or on the major scale; numberless abstractions remind me of the mottos I've seen painted onto uncountable Mexico City walls. The word people is always included in those red or black letters. I remember it as if it preceded my memory altogether: the people of utopia, then the people of unease. I also remember that my first rush of civic feeling, my earliest brush with the country on the other side of my window, was compassion. When I'd leave the house with my parents or the housekeeper (whose old, dusty shoes intensified my discomfort), the disparities, the incongruity of what I saw demanded so much mental effort that it overwhelmed me into muteness. The pieces didn't fit together: that mother with my mother, that girl or boy with me or with my siblings. That's life, my parents would respond when I'd say something about it in the sparse vocabulary of childhood. All the more reason to be grateful for what I had, they'd say. But their response, which remains useful to some extent, did nothing to mitigate the novelty of compassion, the kindest consequence of which was to make me feel virtuous precisely because of the pain I felt at the everyday sight of poor people (I didn't yet call them "the people"). I was going to help them. Outside, I'd ask my mom or dad for coins and run toward the open palm and search the beggar's face for the reward of gratitude. I rarely glimpsed it. There was mostly, I think, vexation. They knew that the alms of a child were symbolic: yet another toy bestowed by her parents. If the beggars were children, the interaction was more intense, though so were the demands; in the end, we'd laugh together, because our truncated sentences felt like a game. My subsequent pride at having fleetingly identified with someone different from myself, an actual poor person, was so powerful that it blunted the sharpest edge of compassion. And then my life would return to its normal spaces, still smarting a bit from the hairline fracture.

3

Compassion ages with you. At first, it's pristine, spontaneous. Then, little by little, it slows into a selective habit,
picky, vulnerable, justifying its weariness with bizarre
phrases like "I only give to children and the elderly," or
"I only give to the elderly: everyone else can get a job,"
or, the most radical of all, "I don't ever give to anyone;
who knows where that money will end up." You convince yourself that pity alone is gift enough and requires
no action to be satisfied. You postpone your indignation, or you train it to kick into gear only in response to
the tumultuous causes that take the form of newspaper
headlines. Money becomes a secret, something deeply
personal, and sharing it amounts to infringing on your
intimate affairs. Unfortunately, beggars don't fit into the
ideology you exercise on literary panels and in parks;
they're too immediate. The solution, you tell yourself,
is as vast as history, as politics itself, and must tempo-
rarily dispense with individuals. Such certainties pacify,
give permission, offer cease-fires so that you can go on
collecting your dues. And suddenly, one day, on the corner of some neighborhood, you realize that your compassion is no longer automatic. Someone approaches to
ask for money and you treat him with irritation, slam
the car door shut, ignore him emphatically. So it goes:
there are lost causes, and this isn't the path for protest

to follow. You hunker back down: the story is slow to set its happenings in motion. The meanwhile belongs to us entirely.

4

Years ago, a makeshift dictionary by the Mexican writer Jorge Ibargüengoitia was published in a cultural supplement. It was a list of impossible words. One—something like *anatileta*—referred to people "who get angry at beggars and accuse them of laziness." I've seen it happen: a form of compassion, matured and politically engaged, that goes around rejecting events too small for recognition. I don't exclude myself from this category. Middle-class Mexican life continues to strike me as so singular that I try to suspend judgment. Childhood in this social sector comes with close-to-home examples, like the archetypal housekeeper I mentioned above. An invisible company, or visible only when summoned; a constant ghost you see, have always seen, out of the corner of your eye. In *Juana de Asbaje*, Amado Nervo remarks that one of the conflicts in seventeenth-century convents was the overpopulation of servants: "In the convents of Mexico . . . there came to be five hundred servants, though there weren't even a hundred nuns, as some had six maids, a privilege extended even to novices." There they must have been, bustling behind the poems of Sor Juana, rustling, rearranging, shaking things out. And here they are still, guardians of our middle-class peace, protectors of our middle-class time.

Against such an ancient, shadow-burdened backdrop, isn't there an inevitable dose of perplexity, of grief? Political experts rebuke me: that's not what this is about. Lacking a dogma, I concede that they're right. They possess structural, institutional knowledge I do not. My notions are pedestrian, surface-level; I dodge bulks and bodies because I'm in a rush, I stop short out of piety, I know how to cultivate my guilt when I slow down, which happens every day. A British friend of mine once remarked, mockingly, "But you come from a country of beggars and maids." And I pushed away his comment as a betrayal of affection. I struggled to shed my annoyance. I thought of my trips to the so-called First World: how the social animal is permitted to relax, to rest. Ambling along impeccable streets, you snub the occasional panhandler without hesitation, board buses and subways as if public transportation were second nature, relax into the transparency of it all. And yet the weightlessness is dizzying, befuddling. Where did it go, the weight of the debt, the guilty corner where your conscience prepares its justifications for thinking one way and living another? As soon as the plane touches down in Mexico City and you peer out the window, the machinery of friction is reinstalled.

You hear the voices—the voices of different neighborhoods, classes, realities—and you resume your accusatory fervor or your inertia, the manners and courtesies that have long let you wander around among so many forms of faulty, extravagant coexistence. The old subconscious refrain repeats automatically in your head: "That's life." And one world blots out the other.

5

Compassion is a net: it halts or softens your fall. It shifts the emphasis of your good intentions when confronted with complex reality, makes you furiously focus on what everyone else isn't doing: the endless list of other people's sins. A great comfort. Carrying on outside are the masks of your putative friends, vicarious commiseration, provisional remedies gorged on feelings, however mixed they may be. Like the distant morning—I was about nine years old—when I rushed outdoors in a fit of near ecstasy to give my decrepit old shoes to another girl. I knelt down, in my red dress with its lacy flounces and white flowers, so that the girl could try on the shoes, so she and her mother and I could share a moment of sudden joy on the sidewalk. But the staging of my gratification-hungry compassion was abruptly ruined: a man in sunglasses cleaved a finger between my legs as he hurried past, hissing "Give me some of that, sweet thing." I dropped the shoes and fled in tears. Back home, the fabric of contrasts reknit itself, bolstered with strength or caution.

I still haven't mastered the art of subterfuge. I guess I prefer the art of uncertainty: its harsh, godless mysticism, its glum, introspective detachment. Sometimes compassion dilates like a long season in an empty place: it dawdles, self-congratulates, reminisces about itself. And sometimes it ruminates, writing "I'm with you, the downtrodden, the poor." It intently studies the creatures it intends to save and lists the broken souls, line after line, sonorously, already glimpsing the public square, the ardent applause. How can you keep from expressing such benevolence? From boasting to your fortunate, apathetic fellows?

According to Hannah Arendt, "The most powerful and perhaps the most devastating passion motivating revolutionaries . . . [is] the passion of compassion." It corrupts, flattens, sparks extreme politics, eliminates individual distances. Outside is the crowd, not the people. Arendt says that revolutions of compassion— meaning all of them since the French Revolution, she adds—seek to establish a new social order rather than to build a new form of government. They're driven by an eloquent empathy with poverty, with the people, a word whose definition was born out of compassion, and the term became the equivalent for misfortune and unhappiness . . . By the same token, the personal legitimacy of those who represented the people and were convinced that all legitimate power must derive from them, could reside only in *ce zèle compatissant* . . . in short, in the capacity to suffer with the 'immense class of the poor,' accompanied by the will to raise compassion to the rank . . . of the highest political virtue.

And to endow the poor with a special, immaculate goodness, lacking any nuance or complexity. To view them as good, genuine, transparent souls, while you—complicated, perverted by possessions, parents, school, well-being—must grapple with the traps and whims of your own opaque personality. And the only way your personality can access this primordial goodness is through the mirror of compassion, where resemblances are discovered or manufactured. It matters little that you always see your own face in the foreground. There's a pinch of love in the revelation: *It's not me, it's the people.* And you save yourself by saving.

Sacrifice is a gentle tangent, because it always happens in the future. I suspect that festive, innocent horizons have already been discarded where I live. Even so, my compassion—which avoids the three rules when it can—continues its everyday exercises, having shed the theatrical body language of the apologist.

6

The present and the past once looked alike. There were the poor of *then*, of *that* today: whole bodies, expressive eyes, respectful palms and murmurs. The compassionate transaction was neat and fruitful; the moral arrangements were firm but not suffocating. Poverty accounted for a considerable part of Mexican folklore and nationalist cliché; it was the color scheme of a drama we all understood to the point of postponing the outcome. And we grew. Warped, if filled with a surprising capacity to imagine the next improvisation. Our famous ingenuity, our cheerful, jovial dance with La Catrina.[6] That seductress.

Until she no longer was. And the collective work was ruined. Now we're called to make metaphors out of dead and mutilated and decapitated and dismembered and missing bodies. Now the new poetics take the floor. If we don't put them on display, we'll be written off as indifferent. That's what I've read in newspapers and

6. The image of a skeleton in flowing skirts and a flowery hat, first depicted in an etching by the printmaker José Guadalupe Posada, now an icon of Mexico's Day of the Dead.

cultural supplements. That's the cry of leaders here and there and everywhere. Even as our childhood extremes endure: beggars and *criadas*, as my grandmother and even the writer Augusto Monterroso pejoratively called them. They let us enact compassion, and they still take care of us with their attentiveness and feather dusters and aprons and liquid cleaning products that smell of prosperity.

Let me be clear: we're horrified. But I think yesterday was the premise of today.

There's too much death in Mexico for us to laugh at it anymore.

13.

ON THE PRODUCTION OF WISDOM

The world of the happy man is different
from that of the unhappy man.

—Wittgenstein

1

Wisdom can't be a feeling, a sensation that seesaws with your mood. It can't be an impulse or a reaction. It can't work just in certain cases. It can't have degrees. It can't exist unless it always does.

2

I don't know what it is. Tradition alludes to ataraxia or apathy, to indifference in the face of any unhappiness— or happiness, for that matter. Someone atavistically wise doesn't let herself be troubled by anything. Which means she's managed to solve a personal problem, a matter of sensibility, not that she changed the world through her attitude. Her motto would have to be *I'm what matters and nothing else concerns me*. She doesn't try to alter what's out of her hands. Such a basic lesson can foster internal harmony and external serenity. I've known people like this, people who take stock of the world and only consider what they can control. I'm sure these are people of privileged temperaments; it's an innate dexterity, not something that can be learned. Wisdom, then, must be a kind of ability, like drawing well or having a pleasant singing voice. A congenital quality you can develop or lose with disuse.

3

In his *Meditations*, Marcus Aurelius wrote about his friend Maximus: "[he] gave the impression of unperverted rectitude rather than that of a reformed character." It's hard to reform if you don't move, if the receptacle is always the same. You'd have to get out, to fix what's broken from outside, then slip back in. A decision won't cut it. Maybe the most unsettling part is that you're not fully the master even of yourself.

4

When I really look at myself, I stop knowing myself. Self-knowledge is always fleeting. It's the result of distraction, never of concentration.

5

According to Marcus Aurelius, a wise man doesn't think about the past or the future: neither time belongs to him. Only the present can be taken away. This should be his sole concern.

6

The past is a memory and the future an expectation or anticipation. Between these two extremes is the peculiar now, which is also where memory and imagination transpire. Today is any hour of the day; yesterday is whatever you can recall, though forgetfulness will always interfere. How can we explain the fact that we're capable of forgetting what we've experienced? Wisdom grapples satisfactorily with these gaping holes. The antidote is usually simple: what can't be resolved should be ignored.

7

The past is the window; the future is the door. The present isn't the architect, but the owner of the house. It can't be owned all at once. Just one room at a time.

8

In *The Enchiridion*, by Epictetus, wisdom means equanimity. It's the stoic principle par excellence, which lets you experience the foulest of external degradations without being affected by them: "[If] you take for your own only that which is your own and view what belongs to others just as it really is, then no one will ever compel you, no one will restrict you; you will find fault with no one, you will accuse no one, you will do nothing against your will; no one will hurt you, you will not have an enemy, nor will you suffer any harm." In short: you'll be the ideal subject of tyranny. That's exactly what Isaiah Berlin's negative liberty means: liberty without circumstances.

9

When I read a book on wisdom, the comfort is immediate, as if the very act of reading solved a problem. Then I shut the book and character imposes itself once more: both my character and the time's. If you understand the advice, you assume you've already applied it or are capable of applying it. But I suspect that wisdom has nothing to do with understanding, isn't something to be learned. It's an instinct.

10

In the *Bhagavad Gita*, Krishna explains to Arjuna that only he who frees himself from desire will attain peace. But desire is a pleasure in itself. Krishna protests: pleasures are addictions and lead to their absence, which is pain. Neither one thing nor the other. Both appetite and the lack of appetite must be eradicated. In return comes blessedness, which isn't a form of content; it contains. I've glimpsed it among noises, when I manage to meditate and the world is the distance between my head and the latest light.

11

Sometimes blessedness is like a cat's sudden entrance into a shadowed space. It's still subject to my interpretation, still metaphorical; it's *like* something. Therefore, according to my books on wisdom, it isn't blessedness, but the image attributed to its absence. If it were real, we wouldn't be able to talk about it. We'd be immersed in its atmosphere.

12

The teachings of the wise tend toward silence. I don't know if there are words after enlightenment. Wise books confirm a path, not a point of arrival, and their instructions produce a kind of wisdom as you follow them. But as soon as you get distracted, nature comes crashing down on you again. And nature, no matter how authentic it may be, is chaotic. And it doesn't obey any virtues. As nearly as I can tell, it behaves randomly when doing good, almost by accident. When it comes to the bad, however, it seems plotted, calculated. A plan. There must be something to conclude from the difference. But conclusions aren't wise; they eliminate all access to curiosity. You should always be able to add another remark. In the kingdom of interpretations, every word is a cog that prompts another meaning. Only a wise person can make the machine stop.

13

My essence, if I have one, is rustic. It sees nature in anthropomorphic terms, as if it were someone, or as if it were inhabited by presences. A tree makes me want to communicate. It must be the divine flaw that precedes reason. As soon as I come into the picture, the bond is smashed.

14

The *Bhagavad Gita* recommends that you live in accordance with your natural tendencies and don't try to become what you're not. At the sign of the slightest deviation, it suggests you meditate, put your head in order: an exercise that simulates the void. Emerging from the trance, you realize that you are what you are and nothing more. The world hasn't changed, just the texture of perception. It's been sapped of its electrical current, the risk of short-circuit. Things no longer revolve around the *I*, but around the concavity you live in; the shell of consciousness, we might say. It's easy to fill it with thoughts, which move faster than the body and in all directions.

15

The trance is like a drug trip. Whatever you saw, whatever you learned on the other side, it stays there, it doesn't come back with you. As if it weren't an experience, but something more like a hallucination, too big to fit in an everyday mind.

16

Every morning, Marcus Aurelius wrote in the second book of his *Meditations*, we must remember that we "shall have to do with meddlers, with the ungrateful, with the insolent, with the crafty, with the envious and the selfish." All such people, he adds, have seen neither the light of good nor the shadow of evil. Which means they aren't following an immutable sequence of principles, but a corroded chain of reactions. Was that what Brodsky meant when he declared, "I have no convictions, I have only nerves"?

17

His *Meditations* must have worked as a kind of nocturnal therapy for Marcus Aurelius, who found himself perpetually at war, always fighting off Germanic armies and expanding imperial borders as he wrote his twelve books or sections. They're the log of an extreme vigilance, a corrective to hubris and vanity. The goal was to behave well—stoically, that is—every single day. And the failure was constant: otherwise, the book never would have existed. "Wilt thou ever, O my soul, be good and single, and one, and naked, more open to view than the body which surrounds thee?"

18

The wise people I've known move lightly. They are wise in part because they don't see themselves as examples, don't impart lessons. They're spontaneous, which an unwise person never is. In the company of a wise person, I feel ashamed of my complexity: I can see that it's an evolutionary limitation, a vestigial organ that gets in my way. Mental labyrinths are exposed as a serious design flaw, useless, dizzying.

19

Wise people lack indecisiveness. They act as if they knew. Or they don't act; they behave with prudence. This infuriates the unwise. How can you abstain from intervention?

20

I don't know if wisdom equates to happiness. I suspect not. There's something anonymous about wise people and everything narcissistic about happy people. Although happiness is a good platform for doing good; you love your neighbor when you're in a good mood. The wise thing, though, would be to do away with moods altogether, shutter the business of emotions. Ataraxia doesn't judge, love, or hate. It doesn't even have opinions.

21

Both the *Meditations* of Marcus Aurelius and the *Bhagavad Gita* are books written in times of war. Maybe wisdom is only attainable amid adversity. Or maybe it's not a form of normal conduct and only stands out in contrast. There's no need for it in the middle of ordinary, everyday life, as there are no major solutions or faults. Such a life seems wise in its lack of extremes.

22

The pride of winning a war must be threatening, because then the conflict of ego begins. According to wise people, this pride must be stamped out, though not necessarily its acts. Ego's gluttony is insatiable, Krishna says, though it's certainly pleasant to indulge. Falling in love with yourself leads to absolute power: you won't compete with yourself or strip yourself of self-love, which feels like a sign of health.

23

From an aesthetic or literary perspective, psychology is downright vulgar. Wise people are above it. Their attributes aren't personal; they have a kind of omniscience. At most, a mere individual can invent an inner life and make it their primary dilemma.

24

Isolation is a condition of wisdom, at least in legends. At the age of thirty, Zarathustra left everything behind and sought shelter on the mountain. There, for an entire decade, "he enjoyed his spirit and solitude." When his heart was enlightened, he decided to descend and impart his teachings on the people: "I want to teach men the sense of their existence." He was so wise that he seemed crazy.

25

Solitude—mine, at least—is unfocused, can't find its own center. A decade on a mountain rustles up ghosts in your monologue. In the struggle to compromise with them, you end up taking your own side. The next step is the urge to explain why you're right. That's why you go down: to speak.

26

Once I went up to a little rooftop studio to learn whatever it is you learn in solitude. I'd stare at the ceiling in search of respite, a glimmer of wisdom. But there were too many mundane voices in my head. According to Zarathustra, two people make for an ideal solitude. It's a riddle I haven't yet solved. In my solitary room, my thinking revealed all the dimensions of its own banality, more Joycean than Nietzschean; erratic, like a captive butterfly. On the mountain, Zarathustra listened to nature and subjected himself to the metamorphoses of the spirit. He came down ready to dance like an authentic god.

27

If solitude is meant for two, it would have to take root between me and myself, which aren't the same. The inner gaze can tell them apart. It's wise because it knows. The fundamental virtue of this communion is that others don't pop up in your head like representatives of someone else's time. It keeps you up at night. Up on his mountain, Zarathustra realized that "one must have all the virtues in order to sleep well."

28

The urban landscape clashes with consciousness in its search for tranquility. You need wilderness to commune. Thoreau moved into his cabin at Walden Pond in 1845, at the age of eighteen, and stayed till 1847. The experiment was a success, judging by the diary he kept during his pastoral stint. Thoreau returned with a message. Wise people usually have messages. They discover goodness when they're alone, which is suspicious. In the end, the world crashes down on them and they can't reaffix the coordinates of contemplation. Goodness becomes a source of ideological anguish.

29

Marcus Aurelius recommended that you "do every deed, speak every word, think every thought in the knowledge that you may end your days at any moment." In other words: "Act as if you could die anytime." Which also exempts you from responsibilities: you're going to die anyway, so there's no problem if you cause harm. There ought to be a midpoint, a dialectic: learning to die means learning to live.

30

Wisdom gauges the consequences, then abstains. I've known wise people who go against themselves for the sake of reaching an outcome that would suit them all. They're well-trained in the art of yielding, of stepping aside, of shrinking themselves down so the space can expand. They don't complain or ask for recognition. Ataraxia has eliminated all traces of vanity. Before bed, after they've turned out the lights, when they think back over their day, I wonder if they congratulate themselves. Virtue must need at least a pinch of pride to nod off at night.

31

I've heard that wise people never complain. But then they must not believe in politics. Excessive tolerance allows for any regime. Complaining may be the only way to participate.

32

In the morning, before I get out of bed, I tell myself: I'll try to be wise today. Which doesn't mean I won't let anything bother me. Still, simple obstacles leave little space for pursuing wisdom. With the first blackout, an animal instinct lurches against the bars of the cage.

33

To Boethius, philosophy proposes the need to reconcile with fate; to accept it, like it or not. If wisdom thrives in hardship or adversity, you're on the right path. The most tangible wisdom is born of unhappiness. The other kind is more like good luck.

34

In the ideal of ataraxia, neither the negative nor the positive sparks a reaction. A wise person remains unruffled by their own and other people's actions. At most, they'll admit a surreptitious slip into melancholy. It's a wise emotion because it's a passive one. Melancholy people tend to be patient, and, as Brodsky notes, they're never hysterical; paralyzed by a mix of skepticism and

fear, they're associated with the kind of stillness that
Krishna prescribes.

35

I know wise people who suffer from outbursts of joy,
and then their particularity is erased: it's in suffering
that they reveal their vocation. Which is quite a punishment. The gestures of happiness are generally vain, possessive. By contrast, sorrow and melancholy are austere,
self-absorbed enough to be mistaken for ataraxia.

36

Certain virtuous people come off as invasive, as if they
were campaigning for something. They aren't wise.
Shaken by the death of God, Zarathustra explains that
the superior man must learn how to be bad, "for the evil
is man's best force." This advice, he adds, is so subtle
that few will understand it. His evil must give off a vital
energy so overwhelming that it looks radiant. The evil
I've seen stands out only in its brutal negligence.

37

The terms are antiquated. Maybe there's already an avant-garde of wisdom, a more modern or technological expression of the unconditional soul. Some wise people have fully assumed the paraphernalia of their age. But their wisdom isn't unlike that of Marcus Aurelius. Which may mean that wisdom and life don't use the same instruments. Or that we're just as rudimentary inside as we were centuries ago.

38

I ask a wise person to teach me to be like her. The wise person studies me, baffled; she has no idea what I'm talking about. I rephrase more clearly: I want to take wisdom lessons. Her perplexity fumbles for words to apologize with. She doesn't know how to teach because she doesn't know what she knows. It's an instinct and it's ineffable. I press her. A kind of stoicism glimmers forth again. Mostly I need to cultivate indifference.

39

Which is much like boredom, which is a keen awareness

of duration, which is a form of anxiety. There must be a place, a proper medium for the wise person to do their thing. In my case, the place still involves types of external support, like cigarettes or cats. When I'm alone, my head replays discordances. Or, in its active, clever mode, it wonders whom to imitate; wisdom, at least, as carbon copy. Maybe that will be enough. But the result is usually just a rough-hewn pantomime.

40

It must be a matter of vocation: not all of us were born to be wise. If we can admit this, then we become mildly wise, and our modesty can be mitigated through our admiration for the truly enlightened.

41

Epictetus writes, "People are not disturbed by events but by opinions of events." The example he cites is death: it's nothing terrible, but the opinion of death is that it's terrible. Silence becomes a positive force: unexplained, things have no mental consequences.

42

I'm superstitious: there are no superfluous examples. We'll never know if Socrates really did learn to die before he died. The riddle of his last words shows that he paid attention to duties and details. More than a garment of memory, Asclepius's rooster is a bet: in the face of transmigration, debts must be settled. You can't have a fowl flapping about in the beyond. What makes this any different from opinions?

43

Wise people say we should always act according to reason, whose orderly flow we can hear in our heads. It urges equilibrium, albeit on a tightrope. What's curious, though, is how often we disobey it, no matter how right reason may be. Its voice is audible, pristine, but it coexists with enemies, hurt feelings, moods. And it takes a certain pleasure in stringing us along, wounding, provoking. But a wise person never succumbs to temptation. Their even temper doesn't guarantee purity; that's only attainable through risk or remorse.

44

Guilt is the best exercise for innocence. Maybe a wise person is so self-sufficient, so mature, so confident that their lack of uncertainty makes them opaque, satisfied. Their behavior isn't dangerous, which means they're spared nothing. They don't accumulate experiences or include them. In fact, they exclude them in the name of rationality, which offers every action an identical shape. Just as it should be: what good can atonement do?

45

On many social occasions, wisdom means not telling the truth; it means pretending. I prefer the melancholy sorts who would rather abstain than lie. You step out into the world with your mask firmly in place; if you complain about how uncomfortable it is, you've succumbed to childish rebellion. "That guy has no feet!" a little boy shouted frankly the other day. The footless man went red and everyone laughed in complicity with the boy. I saw his face. To be wise, you must learn to fake things or silence them, even when drawn-out silence starts to resemble pedantry. "Tell me what you're thinking . . ." "No." Then you read between the lines, and exegesis, or paranoia, begins.

46

I wasn't wise yesterday. Or the day before. But I live with someone who's almost always wise, and a pantheistic cat. They teach me nothing that isn't grounded in the realm of deeds. Which is like learning about time with a calendar. You forget to pay attention.

47

I met another wise person. They smile at disorder and carelessness while I despair, because reality is a crude rehearsal for some scene to be performed later on, without an audience. When it's finally theater, it will play out like something planned ahead of time. For now, I sense confusion where the wise person sees people, humanity. Nothing obstructs their self-love, because equality is a concession of feelings, not a moral value. Wise people love themselves as profoundly as they love others and their smile is kind to the fractures contact can cause. I immediately ascribe them to some mistake of my own. I'm not wise because I insist on being guilty.

48

Wise people don't like to speak poorly of others, which is a total mystery to me, and also a literary obstacle, because it prevents life from being told as a novel. Without flaws, other people are puppets or parables. There's a lot that can go wrong or average; saying nothing about it causes gaps in our knowledge. As if you halted your senses by imposing general welfare, a dictatorship of optimism. That yoke with a slogan: put a good face on it. Someone is always watching us, even in private. The mind is a public place, a tiny polis. That would be the best doctrine against overlooking possible spaces of sensibility, where I fear I may never settle for good. I'm too morbidly curious about the accidents of thought, mine and other people's. It skids past the "here and now," trying to escape into thoughts of me or itself. It never becomes the center of its center.

49

It happened last night amid murmuring voices. One told me again that I need to learn the supreme lesson of simplicity. It's unquestionably problematic to see yourself as more complicated than the world. Inside, you should be transparent and accessible and the walls of the corridors leading outside must never be smudged. The haze is caused by confinement and perspective.

50

I read in an essay that the present is overrated and we should defend the art of disappointment and digression. How to advocate for pessimism? Requesting loyalty to the present is like demanding that faith be grounded in a tautology. The inevitable is here, if only from instant to instant. Disappointment invaded me before expectation did. By now, I suppose I've developed a certain aptitude for transforming it into a spiritual resource. The present isn't welcoming, unless you add some aimless nostalgia to it. When I digress, all directions appear before me: twists and turns and nooks and crannies where judgment hides to keep from having to choose. The present flings you into the open air, promising that wisdom will come once you've dominated the obvious.

51

According to William Hazlitt, good people are the most hypocritical; bad people are the most generous. Good people care about nothing but themselves: they don't get hot and bothered, don't get indignant, don't get riled up. Bad people, by contrast, strain against the circumstances and want to rectify offenses. This, of course, makes them angry, vulnerable, and unpleasant to others. Behind the cleverness, there must be a clear distinction: the truly good and the truly bad. It would be comforting to conclude that a wise person, deep down, is an utterly selfish person, and that their opposite, the unwise person, answers to the stirrings of a noble soul. And so we'd have to act through paradoxes and protect ourselves from any affection that distracted us from apathy.

52

Proper nouns are a disservice to nature. Communion transpires in total anonymity. This often befalls wise people on beaches, when they contemplate the ocean and make professions about the future. I observe them observing and long to emulate them. But I tend to saddle myself with deadweights: *I* is one of them. Such interference keeps the ocean from comfortably revealing itself and I join the storyline of the spectacle.

53

Maybe I'll become wise if I act like it. At first, I'd follow the rules to a T, obeying the protocol until I'd successfully eliminated anything original. My goal would be to replace my personhood with a series of conventions that would unravel the snares of inner life. My dreams and unconscious would be granted all the rights of the eccentric mind.

54

I'll start early tomorrow. The first step is to cultivate indifference. The second is to forget I'm cultivating it. In the space between the two, there will be discoveries I'll have to accept with total neutrality. If I get ahead of myself, I break the rule. If I imagine them, I'm committing an act of arrogance, as if their genesis were up to me. There are litanies in the air that only the alienated can discern. I hope to transcribe them. So that the defectors have a score of their own and I can soften my urge to dig deeper: what does identity sound like? Once erased, wisdom sands the walls and paints them white. You can live there almost every day. Jot it down, spread the word: the real remedy is to embark from no one.

Works Cited

Arendt, Hannah. *On Revolution*. London: Penguin Books, 1991.

Aurelius, Marcus. *The Meditations of the Emperor Marcus Aurelius Antoninus*. Translated by George W. Chrystal. London: S.C. Brown and Company, 1902.

Cioran. E. M. *Anathemas and Admirations*. Translated by Richard Howard. New York: Arcade, 2012.

Dostoevsky, Fyodor. *Notes from the Underground*. Translated by Constance Garnett. Garden City, NY: Dover Thrift Editions, 1992.

Epictetus. *The Enchiridion*. Translated by Thomas W. Higgins. New York: Liberal Arts Press, 1948.

Hesse, Hermann. *Demian*. Translated by Stanley Appelbaum. Garden City, NY: Dover Thrift Editions, 2000.

La Rochefoucauld, François, duc de. *Reflections; or Sentences and Moral Maxims*. Translated by J. W. Willis Bund and J. Hain Friswell. London: Simpson Low, Son, and Marston, 1871.

Sartre, Jean-Paul. *Nausea*. Translated by Lloyd Alexander. New York: New Directions, 1964.

Tedi López Mills is one of Mexico's foremost poets writing today. She is the author of ten books of poetry and two essay collections, several of which have received national literary prizes. An English edition of her poetry collection *Against the Current*, in translation by Wendy Burk, was published by Phoneme in 2016. She lives in Mexico City, Mexico.

Robin Myers is a Mexico City–based translator and poet. She was among the winners of the 2019 Poems in Translation Contest (Words Without Borders / Academy of American Poets) and is an alumna of the Banff International Literary Translation Centre. Her translation of Mariana Spada's *The Law of Conservation* will be published by Deep Vellum in 2023.

Thank you all
for your support.
We do this for you,
and could not do
it without you.

DEEP
VELLUM

PARTNERS

FIRST EDITION MEMBERSHIP
Anonymous (9)
Donna Wilhelm

TRANSLATOR'S CIRCLE
Ben & Sharon Fountain
Meriwether Evans

PRINTER'S PRESS MEMBERSHIP
Allred Capital Management
Robert Appel
Charles Dee Mitchell
Cullen Schaar
David Tomlinson & Kathryn Berry
Jeff Leuschel
Judy Pollock
Loretta Siciliano
Lori Feathers
Mary Ann Thompson-Frenk & Joshua Frenk
Matthew Rittmayer
Nick Storch
Pixel and Texel
Social Venture Partners Dallas
Stephen Bullock

AUTHOR'S LEAGUE
Christie Tull
Farley Houston
Jacob Seifring
Lissa Dunlay
Stephen Bullock
Steven Kornajcik
Thomas DiPiero

PUBLISHER'S LEAGUE
Adam Rekerdres
Christie Tull
Justin Childress
Kay Cattarulla
KMGMT
Olga Kislova

EDITOR'S LEAGUE
Amrit Dhir
Brandon Kennedy
Dallas Sonnier
Garth Hallberg
Greg McConeghy
Linda Nell Evans
Mary Moore Grimaldi
Mike Kaminsky
Patricia Storace
Ryan Todd
Steven Harding
Suejean Kim

Symphonic Source
Wendy Belcher

READER'S LEAGUE
Caitlin Baker
Caroline Casey
Carolyn Mulligan
Chilton Thomson
Cody Cosmic & Jeremy Hays
Jeff Waxman
Joseph Milazzo
Kayla Finstein
Kelly Britson
Kelly & Corby Baxter
Marian Schwartz & Reid Minot
Marlo D. Cruz Pagan
Maryam Baig
Peggy Carr
Susan Ernst

ADDITIONAL DONORS
Alan Shockley
Amanda & Bjorn Beer
Andrew Yorke
Anonymous (10)
Anthony Messenger
Ashley Milne Shadoin
Bob & Katherine Penn
Brandon Childress
Charley Mitcherson
Charley Rejsek
Cheryl Thompson
Chloe Pak
Cone Johnson
CS Maynard
Daniel J. Hale
Daniela Hurezanu
Dori Boone-Costantino
Ed Nawotka
Elizabeth Gillette
Erin Kubatzky
Ester & Matt Harrison
Grace Kenney
Hillary Richards
JJ Italiano
Jeremy Hughes
John Darnielle
Julie Janicke Muhsmann
Kelly Falconer
Laura Thomson
Lea Courington
Leigh Ann Pike
Lowell Frye
Maaza Mengiste

EMBREY FAMILY
FOUNDATION

ALLRED
CAPITAL MANAGEMENT
of
RAYMOND JAMES®

ADDITIONAL DONORS, CONT'D

Mark Haber
Mary Cline
Maynard Thomson
Michael Reklis
Mike Soto
Mokhtar Ramadan
Nikki & Dennis Gibson
Patrick Kukucka
Patrick Kutcher
Rev. Elizabeth & Neil Moseley
Richard Meyer

Scott & Katy Nimmons
Sherry Perry
Sydneyann Binion
Stephen Harding
Stephen Williamson
Susan Carp
Susan Ernst
Theater Jones
Tim Perttula
Tony Thomson

SUBSCRIBERS

Margaret Terwey
Ben Fountain
Gina Rios
Elena Rush
Courtney Sheedy
Caroline West
Brian Bell
Charles Dee Mitchell
Cullen Schaar
Harvey Hix
Jeff Lierly
Elizabeth Simpson

Nicole Yurcaba
Jennifer Owen
Melanie Nicholls
Alan Glazer
Michael Doss
Matt Bucher
Katarzyna Bartoszynska
Michael Binkley
Erin Kubatzky
Martin Piñol
Michael Lighty
Joseph Rebella

Jarratt Willis
Heustis Whiteside
Samuel Herrera
Heidi McElrath
Jeffrey Parker
Carolyn Surbaugh
Stephen Fuller
Kari Mah
Matt Ammon
Elif Ağanoğlu

AVAILABLE NOW FROM DEEP VELLUM

SHANE ANDERSON · *After the Oracle* · USA

MICHÈLE AUDIN · *One Hundred Twenty-One Days* · translated by Christiana Hills · FRANCE

BAE SUAH · *Recitation* · translated by Deborah Smith · SOUTH KOREA

MARIO BELLATIN · *Mrs. Murakami's Garden* · translated by Heather Cleary · *Beauty Salon* · translated by David Shook · MEXICO

EDUARDO BERTI · *The Imagined Land* · translated by Charlotte Coombe · ARGENTINA

CARMEN BOULLOSA · *Texas: The Great Theft* · *Before* · *Heavens on Earth*
translated by Samantha Schnee · Peter Bush · Shelby Vincent · MEXICO

MAGDA CARNECI · *FEM* · translated by Sean Cotter · ROMANIA

LEILA S. CHUDORI · *Home* · translated by John H. McGlynn · INDONESIA

MATHILDE CLARK · *Lone Star* · translated by Martin Aitken · DENMARK

SARAH CLEAVE, ed. · *Banthology: Stories from Banned Nations* ·
IRAN, IRAQ, LIBYA, SOMALIA, SUDAN, SYRIA & YEMEN

LOGEN CURE · *Welcome to Midland: Poems* · USA

ANANDA DEVI · *Eve Out of Her Ruins* · translated by Jeffrey Zuckerman · MAURITIUS

PETER DIMOCK · *Daybook from Sheep Meadow* · USA

CLAUDIA ULLOA DONOSO · *Little Bird,* translated by Lily Meyer · PERU/NORWAY

RADNA FABIAS · *Habitus* · translated by David Colmer · CURAÇAO/NETHERLANDS

ROSS FARRAR · *Ross Sings Cheree & the Animated Dark: Poems* · USA

ALISA GANIEVA · *Bride and Groom* · *The Mountain and the Wall*
translated by Carol Apollonio · RUSSIA

FERNANDA GARCIA LAU · *Out of the Cage* · translated by Will Vanderhyden · ARGENTINA

ANNE GARRÉTA · *Sphinx* · *Not One Day* · *In/concrete* · translated by Emma Ramadan · FRANCE

JÓN GNARR · *The Indian* · *The Pirate* · *The Outlaw* · translated by Lytton Smith · ICELAND

GOETHE · *The Golden Goblet: Selected Poems* · *Faust, Part One*
translated by Zsuzsanna Ozsváth and Frederick Turner · GERMANY

SARA GOUDARZI · *The Almond in the Apricot* · USA

NOEMI JAFFE · *What are the Blind Men Dreaming?* · translated by Julia Sanches & Ellen Elias-Bursac · BRAZIL

CLAUDIA SALAZAR JIMÉNEZ · *Blood of the Dawn* · translated by Elizabeth Bryer · PERU

PERGENTINO JOSÉ · *Red Ants* · MEXICO

TAISIA KITAISKAIA · *The Nightgown & Other Poems* · USA

SONG LIN · *The Gleaner Song: Selected Poems* · translated by Dong Li · CHINA

JUNG YOUNG MOON · *Seven Samurai Swept Away in a River* · *Vaseline Buddha*
translated by Yewon Jung · SOUTH KOREA

KIM YIDEUM · *Blood Sisters* · translated by Ji yoon Lee · SOUTH KOREA

JOSEFINE KLOUGART · *Of Darkness* · translated by Martin Aitken · DENMARK

YANICK LAHENS · *Moonbath* · translated by Emily Gogolak · HAITI

FORTHCOMING FROM DEEP VELLUM